PROFILES OF INTEGRITY

4

Real People Who Demonstrated Godly Character

Marilyn Boyer &
Grace Tumas Ehrman

Master Books First Printing: January 2026

Master Books, P.O. Box 726, Green Forest, AR 72638

Master Books® is a division of
the New Leaf Publishing Group, LLC.

ISBN: 978-1-68344-432-9
ISBN: 978-1-61458-951-8 (digital)

All Scripture verses are from the King James Version of the Bible.

Please consider requesting that a copy of this volume be purchased by your local library system.

Printed in the United States of America

Please visit our website for other great titles:
www.masterbooks.com

For information regarding promotional opportunities, please contact the publicity department at pr@nlpg.com.

PROFILES OF INTEGRITY

4

Real People
Who Demonstrated
Godly Character

Marilyn Boyer &
Grace Tumas Ehrman

Credits

Thanks to the following people for their indispensable help in writing Portraits of Integrity: Grace Tumas Ehrman, for her sensitive and colorful portrayal of these heroes in writing their stories.

Mary Ann Edman who, with help from her husband Ed, produced the layout and design, along with other beautiful graphic effects. Thanks, Mary Ann, for your commitment to excellence! And Judy Saunders, Krystyn Walker, and Grace Boyer for their proofreading work.

Chronological Table of Contents

Table of Contents by Character Quality

Introduction

Some stories are just too good to be lost to history. They need to be told and retold and used to inspire the current generation to accomplish mighty feats in our day. This volume is especially moving to me, as one of the authors. I personally met and interviewed two of the men written about and had a first-person account of one of the others. World War 2 is chock-full of amazing stories of sacrifice and determination.

Be prepared to be inspired by the lives of these brave men who met challenging circumstances with resolve and character. They were faced with life and death situations and came through, leaving for us shining examples of persistence under fire. They all had jobs to accomplish and risked their own safety for the good of others.

One of those that has served to affect and inspire many is the story of Jacob DeShazer. Because one man chose to practice forgiveness to his torturers thousands of Japanese people came to a saving knowledge of Jesus Christ. Consider Cecil Breeden who was under thick enemy fire but did his duty without thinking of his own safety, administering medical care to the many wounded on D-Day. Or Eddie Simpson who willingly gave his life that others might live and advance the cause of freedom. God uses what at first seem to be terrible circumstances in our lives to advance the Gospel of Jesus Christ. Let us remember when we face hard times to look for the courage to stand strong and be used of God in ways we could never have thought of. When you read these true accounts of real people, look for evidence of how God used the performance of their duty to save lives and advance His kingdom.

Marilyn Boyer

Basic to our democratic civilization are the principles and convictions that have bound us together as a nation. Among these are personal liberty, human rights, and the dignity of man. All these have their roots in a deeply held religious faith – in a belief in God.

—President Dwight D. Eisenhower,
the Address at U.S. Naval Academy
Commencement, June 4, 1958

Honor

DEFINITION

Viewing and treating others as
a special creation of God

MEMORY VERSE

Honour all men. Love the brotherhood.
Fear God. Honour the king.
I Peter 2:17

The Black Baron

General Pyotr Wrangel

The Russian Civil War, Crimea
October 1920

October 16, 1920. An east wind came in the night, steadily blowing the salt water from the Sivash Marsh. Ordinarily too deep to cross on foot, the marshes formed the last line of defense. But not tonight. And in the darkness, a godless army, wearing red stars on their caps, crossed over onto dry land. Now they were marching, and nothing could stop them.

Thick fog crept up from the sea, blotting out objects close at hand and bringing with it a chill of loneliness. On the hills above Perekop, a handful of

General Pyotr Wrangel in 1920

worn-out defenders battled the cold. They had been fighting and retreating for three days without food or sleep. The men of the White Army lay huddled in shell holes crisscrossed with twisted jumbles of barbed wire. Officers wore shabby grey greatcoats with the insignia drawn on in black ink. Some of them stuffed straw into their shirts to keep warm. As the sun spread slowly across the horizon, they could see the landscape dusted with silver hoarfrost. In the grey dawn, the Red Army communists came over the earthworks like an avalanche. Sixty-thousand strong and outnumbering the White Army three to one, the Red Army scrambled up the ravine. The White Army responded with the crack-crack of rifle fire. Shrapnel burst with white puffs left and right, spitting bits of snow like millions of pine-needles into soldiers' faces. Then they struggled back through the barbed wire to the second, unfinished row of trenches.

Forty-two-year-old General Pyotr Wrangel listened grimly to the radio reports at army headquarters. His tall slender figure, in a tight-fitting black cherkeska coat with cartridge-pockets sewn on the chest, grew rigid as he sent out a message for help.

His fine face with its clipped mustache contorted for a brief moment in anguish. He had no troops left under his command.

When Vladimir Lenin's Communist Party seized control of the Russian Provisional Government in 1917, the fate of the country remained undecided. Who would win: a ruthless, left-wing party determined to subordinate all to its atheistic control, or groups of men dedicated to the right of the people to choose their own representative democracy?

The White Army fought through blinding blizzards and suffocating heat. They had starved and survived. Last year, a year of miracles and victories, they came within 100 miles of taking the Communist capital, Moscow. Then the American and British forces pulled out. Without aid, the little army began backing southward towards the Crimea, pursued by relentless, pitiless intent. With resistance crumbling across the country, Baron General Pyotr Wrangel's White Army stood as the last threat to Communism.

They called him "The Black Baron" because of the black cherkeska (long coat) that he wore. They wrote songs about him. They feared his courage, charisma, and honor.

Wrangel stared out the window as darkness closed in again. The temperature stood at twenty degrees below zero. Water froze in the pumps in the street. All through the night, he kept sending desperate messages to General Kutepov, ordering him to rush to the aid of the defenders at the Sivash March. By October 20, whole divisions were surrendering. The Red Army gleefully rode trains piled high with booty, prisoners, and ammunition. The whole front had collapsed. Reflecting on that time he later said:

The Black Baron in his cherkeska

"The dead weight of failure was crushing my heart. Again and again I asked myself if it had not been my fault. Had I foreseen everything? Had all my calculations been accurate?"

When he took over the army in March, it seemed a lost cause. Abandoned by its commander-in-chief, it had become a rapidly degenerating army swelled by thousands of refugee women and children. During weeks of incredible hard work, he had organized them into a new army, fed them with words of honor and courage, giving them the hope that they could win again. During the past eight months, they beat back superior forces and took back ground they thought they would never walk on again. But in sweeping cavalry moves, the enemy had gobbled up all of Northern Caucasia, won with much blood and sweat that last summer. Now, boxed into a narrow strip of beach, White Army would be cut to pieces. Their only hope lay in escape. General Abramov's Cossacks threw themselves on the enemy's flank, breaking open a way to the Crimea and the sea. Fighting every step through the Perekop Pass, the White Army managed to slip through.

On October 22nd, General Wrangel held a meeting of the local government in Sevastopol. He concealed the worst of the situation in order to prevent panic behind the lines. Putting on a cheerful face, he forced himself to attend a musical party that evening. His chest tight and throbbing with pain, his mind remained with his men at the Sivash Marsh. He described the desperate situation: "The storm was approaching; our fate was hanging by a thread; we had to strain every moral and intellectual force. The slightest irresolution, the most insignificant mistake, and all would be lost."

Meanwhile, he organized every hospital, train, and dozens of ships capable of carrying 20,000 men. He had to evacuate the able men and the wounded, as well as old men and women carting luggage, pianos, lap dogs, and children. Seeing the end in sight, he planned each detail to avoid chaos. As his calm and desperate plans went forth, reports still bled through from the front. Several units had rallied on their own and taken back their positions from the enemy. But they were too weak to hold them for long. Throughout that last long night, men frantically shoveled coal into the furnaces of the transport-boats as the Red Army drew nearer.

November 2nd:

Russian exiles leaving Crimea, 1920

They could hear General Wrangel pacing the floor upstairs in the empty palace on the shores of the Black Sea. He looked haggard, deep lines circling his eyes. He was making his last preparations. A staff officer waiting below heard his long, regular strides in the ballroom and then a terrible crashing sound. He rushed upstairs. In the twilight, Wrangel had laid the topographical maps, raised bumps showing their units and positions, on the floor and walked the length of them, trampling them flat. When the Bolsheviks arrived, they would find nothing but crumpled scraps of paper. Staring down with tired grey eyes, he could see lights bobbing like Japanese lanterns in the harbor. Almost 100,000 men, women, and children milled in the darkened town like sheep, waiting to board the boats. And there were not enough boats. *I will bring you out alive*, he had promised. And he would keep that promise if he died.

November 3rd:

The massive operation went into action. The cold spell had broken. Gulls wheeled above them in the blue sky with shrieking cries. Wrangel felt sweat trickle down his face as he watched the shore in a pink haze. The embarkation went on through the early morning hours. No one pushed or shoved. They boarded quietly, in an orderly fashion. French, Turkish, and Greek fishing smacks floated out of the sea, pulling refugees aboard. Wrangel's voice rang across the quay: "We are going into exile; we are not going as beggars with outstretched hands, but with our heads held high, conscious of having done our duty to the end." People crowded around him, kissing his hands and weeping. At 2 p.m. he received a radio message from the chief of the fleet: "Embarkation finished. Everyone on board to the last soldier."

His shoulders lifted and fell with relief. In a brilliant piece of organization, the vast flotilla set sail across the Bay to freedom, like Moses and his people. They had outrun the Red Army, who remained a day behind. "I felt an immense weight fall from my mind. God had helped me to do my duty. He would bless our journey into the unknown." He was the last man to board the ship.

Evacuation of Novorossiysk

The post-war years remained ones of constant struggles for Wrangel. Detained in wretched camps by the French on the isle of Lemnos, he not only kept up the men's fighting spirit and skills, but he fought to gain rights, recognition, and jobs for thousands of his people. He answered hundreds of letters personally and helped poor refugees out of his own dwindling pocket. He even took in a disabled Cossack soldier without any relatives who lived under the staircase in his crowded house. He organized an aid society that still exists today. During 1920–1926, he kept the army knit together, intending to return and take up the fight again. Having won their love, respect and admiration, General Wrangel gained the status of a Christian knight among his men.

The Communists still feared him. They knew that he would return and fight if possible. They now took ruthless steps to eliminate the man they viewed as a threat. In April 1928, a Soviet sailor, brother of Wrangel's butler, appeared at the family's three-story brick home in Belgium. He spent all day in the kitchen and then left abruptly. All at once, the General fell violently ill as if poisoned. Doctors could not find what caused the high fever and hallucinations.

His brain played the last battle scenes in the Crimea over and over, unwinding like shaky old movie reels. He kept solving mathematical problems, drawing up charts and commands. He struggled to stand up, to give orders, to lead again. Raw dawn flowed over the steppe, cold and clear as chloroform. In the distance, he could see the flat roofs and chimneys of Sevastopol. Shadows of war raced like wild horses through his dreams.

Saying goodbye to the sharp, sweet taste of Russian air and winter hurrying from the mountains, he boards the *Waldek Rousseau*, his tall grey figure with its high sheepskin hat casting a long shadow on the water. "Night is falling. The stars are gleaming in the darkening sky; the sea is all a-twinkle. The lonely lights on my native shore grow fainter, and then vanish altogether, one after the other. And now the last one fades from my sight." Today he would leave forever, and the city that he had loved and hated would go away into the misty places of memory, the haunt of seagulls and wild horses, from which there is no going and no return.

For thirty-eight days he suffered. Then at 9 a.m. on April 25, 1928, Gencral Wrangel died in his sleep. He was forty-nine years old. His last thought was for the welfare of his people.

He had lived up to the spirit of his memoirs: *Always with Honor.* He had made a promise to the people under his protection to lead them to safety and freedom and he had kept it.

History, which knows no favoritism, will tell the importance of our struggle, the capacity of our sacrifices. It will know that the fight we carried on for the love of our country, for the resurrection of Russia as a nation, was indeed at the same time to safeguard the culture of Europe, the struggle for an age-long civilization, for the defence of Europe against the Red terror.

—General Pyotr Wrangel,
from his book,
Always with Honor

Questions

1. Against what were General Wrangel's men fighting?
2. Why did Wrangel's men call him the "Black Baron"?
3. How was the war going at this time?
4. What was the only hope for his men?
5. What kind of preparations did he have to make for successful evacuation?
6. What promise had General Wrangel made to the people?
7. What did he say to encourage them?
8. Was his plan successful?
9. How did his army feel about him? How did the Communists feel about him?
10. What led to his death?
11. How had he succeeded in treating his people with honor?
12. Name some people to whom you could show honor.
13. Do you have veterans in your family? In what ways can you honor veterans?

Punctuality

DEFINITION

Being prompt in all commitments, honoring the time of others

MEMORY VERSE

Walk in wisdom toward them that are without, redeeming the time.

Colossians 4:5

Tracks

Gunnar Kaasen

Nome, Alaska

February 1925

Balto lifted his head. He sniffed the air, delicately arching his tongue. He tasted snow. The sharp tang sent a shiver through his body though he wasn't cold. It tickled his fur, sifting like dry, gritty sand between the straps of the sled harness and his body. All around him the world was icebound. He strained forward, seeing nothing but the barren sweep of the Alaskan tundra stretching into the early arctic twilight. Above, behind, swirling in the air around him, he could hear Gunnar Kaasen's hoarse voice.

The voice pulled him forward. Again and again.

January 20, 1925

A radio telegraph signal flashed across Alaska to Anchorage: *Nome calling. . . Nome calling. . . We have an outbreak of diphtheria. . . No Serum . . . Urgently need help. . . Nome calling. . . Nome calling. . .*

Diphtheria was sweeping through Nome like wildfire. Villages huddled like gnomes on the edge of the world. A child lay gasping, mucus closing over its lungs. Three Inuit children had died already. Desperate, Dr. Welch tapped out a message to Anchorage almost 1,000 miles away.

The message came back:

Fresh serum available here . . . Airplanes standing by to fly to Nome. . .

Anchorage located 300,000 units of precious antitoxin in a railway hospital—enough to save the children's lives and prevent an epidemic. But the lone aircraft in Anchorage lay in pieces for repair. Snow continued to fall heavily outside. As the temperature dropped below zero, ice congealed on the blades, jamming the motor. The plane refused to start. The officials looked at each other. They needed dogs. Only the experienced teams of mushers who ran the Iditarod Trail could break through to Nome in time. They shipped the package by train to Nenana.

At the station, "Wild Bill" Shannon grabbed the twenty-pound package, lashed it to his sled and took off. When he started, it was 30 degrees below zero. Then it began to drop to 35 degrees. Then 40 . . . then 45. As the arctic blackness settled in, it reached 50 degrees below zero. Shannon pressed on, hearing only the whooshing of runners over the snow, the sound of the dogs' panting. Fifty-two miles later, at Tolovana, he handed the serum over to Edgar Kalland.

January 28th

Kalland headed into the wilderness, passing the package to Dan Green at Manley Hot Springs. Green sped with the serum into the darkness, averaging an incredible nine miles per hour, until he stumbled into Fish Lake. Johnny Folger managed twenty-six miles before turning it over to Sam Joseph. Fresh snow began to fall as Joseph's frozen fingers slapped the package into Titus Nikolai's hands. Nikolai took off. The wind-chill increased, causing whiteouts. And still the mushers pushed on. Rugged men, Native American, Inuit, and Caucasian, huddled at the relay points to dash on with the medicine for the children at Nome.

January 30th

The young, newly-wed Alaskan Athabaskan, George Nollner, sang Athabascan love songs as he disappeared into the darkness. The songs kept him warm, beating in his blood as the dogs charged ahead. Soon it was time for the next team. During Charlie Evan's bleak, thirty-mile stretch, two of his dogs dropped dead on their feet. They had frozen solid. Evans strapped his own body to the traces and began leading the dragging sled. He made it to the next relay post alive. Jackscrew, a member of the Koyukuk, covered another forty miles, while Irishman Myles Gonangnan did the same.

January 31st

They didn't stop for rest or food. Russian Inuit Henry Ivanoff embarked from Shaktolik for what he knew was the most dangerous stretch of the run. Half a mile up the trail, one of his dogs veered off the road to chase a reindeer. Ivanoff jumped into the snarling pack as dogs, traces, and sled tangled with each other. Glancing up, he saw the Norwegian Leonhard Seppala, with his famous Siberian husky, Togo, racing down the trail. Seppala, one of the greatest mushers in the Alaskan territory, had started out from Nome, 150 miles away, to meet the relay. Storms buffeted them as Seppala approached the treacherous, frozen Norton Sound. It lay before him like the sea, grey and menacing,

Togo

its banks rippled with ice. He didn't know what the middle was like or if they could touch it without breaking through.

Seppala gazed across the Sound. He could go around it, which would take him miles out of his way. Or he could try to cross it. Seppala chose the shortest route. Seawater crashed around them. The ice creaked and groaned, threatening to crack under them any second. Water was soaking over the sled runners as Togo, footing his way among the jagged ice floes, led them up the other side. Three hours later, the ice broke up in Norton Sound with a noise like gunshots.

February 1st

The serum was now passed from Norwegian to Norwegian. Leonhard Seppala handed the package to Charlie Olsen, who gave it to Gunnar Kaasen—the man destined to make the last, hazardous dash to Nome. At Bluff, Kaasen stared into the horizon with crinkled eyes. A storm kicked up puffs of snow, sweeping it across the tundra like billowing white sand. Stooping over Seppala's team, Kaasen chose one of the dogs to lead him out of Bluff.

White breath clouded his face. It was hard to talk and the men communicated with jerks of the head. Then the lead harness slipped over Balto's dark head and tightened around his thick neck. One white-splashed paw lifted, tense and trembling. His ears pricked forward. The intelligent brown eyes gleamed.

He was chosen. Balto felt the man's steady hands on the traces. They had never let him in front before. They kept him back, letting the big dog, Togo, toss his head in front. Today, he would face his first great test. He had never been a leader. Never had to sniff the wind or dig out a trail on his own. He could smell the storm coming. But Kaasen didn't think it was severe.

Gunnar Kaasen and Balto

Balto lurched into the wind. It was more than 50 degrees below zero. Gusting winds slapped them with snow that cut like shards of glass. Battling the gale-force wind and breaking a path through four-foot-high drifts, the man and 13 dogs forced their way to the river. It was a total whiteout. Kaasen was silent now, and he couldn't see his hand in front of his face. Balto plunged on, guided by Kaasen and instinct. Suddenly, the sled twisted sideways, sliding into the Topkok River and Kaasen falling. Balto and the other dogs struggled, pulling the sled up the cliff by sheer force.

When the team swooshed into the Safety Shelter, they found the next relay driver sound asleep, unprepared to finish the journey. No one had expected Kaasen and his team to live through the blizzard. Now, they would have to take the serum twice as far.

Kassen looked at Balto, gauging his strength. Kaasen crouched and lifted the dogs' paws, testing the soft pads for cuts and wounds. When the Norwegian rose, and stepped onto the runners of the dog sled, the dogs knew instinctively, they would go on.

Winds accelerated as they left the shelter. As they crossed the tundra, a gust of wind lifted dogs and sled into the air, hurling them into a snowdrift. The huskies landed in a tangle of harness and fur. Kaasen, struggling with the sled, suddenly went down on his knees. The man look desperately from side to side. The serum was gone. Kaasen scrabbled frantically in the snow with his bare hands. Then his stiff fingers closed over the little package.

February 2nd

At 5:30 a.m. Kaasen and his team, staggering and frozen to the bone, drove past the silent streets and wooden house-fronts of Nome. They had made most of the run in total darkness. The families of the saved children crowded round him, thanking Kaasen with tears in their eyes. But Kaasen stooped to the stocky black dog with bright brown eyes. "Balto," he said, "should have his share of fame." More than twenty drivers and their teams participated in the 674-mile race to Nome that took just six days: a feat that mushers consider a world record.

Balto and Gunnar Kaasen demonstrated punctuality by driving themselves beyond the call of duty to get the serum to the children on time.

...I want to speak of that classic, heroic dog-team relay that carried antitoxin for the suffering, dying people of the little city of Nome away out there on the coast of the Bering Sea..

... we should always remember that the rapid and successful carrying of this antitoxin to Nome was due as much to the unknown drivers and the unknown dogs fighting their way through the blizzards over the lonely, dead ice desert, each doing his part to make the final victory possible, and that they deserve equal credit with those whose names came through in the news dispatches.

—Comments placed into the United States Senate's Congressional Record, page 3114; February 6, 1925

Questions

1. What was the emergency situation in Nome, Alaska?
2. Why couldn't they just put the medicine on a plane or train?
3. The weather changed about the time Kaasen and Balto set out. How severe did it become?
4. What happened at Point Safety?
5. How many miles did Balto run?
6. What mishaps occurred along the way?
7. How did Gunnar and Balto demonstrate punctuality?
8. What happened to the citizens of Nome?
9. Does time matter? If you are supposed to do something by a certain time, should you take it seriously?
10. Is there something you tend to be late for? What steps can you take to remedy the situation?

Forgiveness

DEFINITION

Picturing how Jesus died on the Cross for my sins so that God's love can flow through me to others who have wronged me

MEMORY VERSE

Forbearing one another,
and forgiving one another,
if any man have a quarrel against any:
even as Christ forgave you, so also do ye.
Colossians 3:13

Angel's Wings

Jacob DeShazer

World War II, Japan
December 1941

He heard the sound of planes before he saw them. At 7:49 on the morning of Sunday, December 7, 1941, Japanese planes led by 39-year-old flying ace Mitsuo Fuchida, honed in on Pearl Harbor, Hawaii, through the mists. Fuchida, sporting a small black mustache, felt his heart squeeze with pride. He was not a *kamikaze*—Japanese pilots who chose to go down with their planes. Selected by the government to fly this special mission and with 49 bombers under his command, Fuchida knew little of the men he had

Japanese planes attack Pearl Harbor

been sent to destroy. Only that they were enemies. Glancing out of the pilot's window to his left, he saw 51 dive bombers cruising at an altitude of 200 meters above him. Slightly below him to his right roared 40 torpedo planes in shark formation. At his back, covering the attack, hovered an additional 43 bombers. Visibility cleared over Honolulu.

In the port waters, heavy with dark silhouettes, battleships and cruisers were neatly arranged in the seemingly safe harbor. As Fuchida gave the signal to attack, bombs dropped on Ford Island, Hickam Field, and Wheeler Field, blowing heavy bombers stationed on the ground into the air. Peering through binoculars, Fuchida ordered all ten of his squadrons to fall into a single line of attack. Just then, the anti-aircraft aboard the nearer ships burst into orange flame. They were shooting back. Fuchida's plane shook with the impact. Without hesitation, he dropped his bombs. Far below, the ships *Utah*, *The West Virginia,* and *Nevada* bunched like sitting ducks. The bombs looked like seeds falling. Then there came a white flash and a jolting explosion. Waterspouts from the bay shot into the air. Red-black smoke ballooned like mushroom clouds 1,000 feet into the air, darkening the sky. Four or five ships were on fire. Others listed,

Sergeant Jacob DeShazer

huge gashes torn in their sides as water poured in and wounded seaman thrashed, trying to keep from drowning in holds rapidly filling with water. Some of the American pilots tried desperately to get their planes off the ground. Fuchida watched in admiration as they flew in, trying to get a hit at the Japanese aircraft. An hour after the first attack, the second wave of planes swooped in. The entire seaplane base was a mass of flames. Fuchida, noting the damage, turned his bomber back towards Admiral Nagumo's fleet, where he urged a third attack. The Admiral, ignoring his suggestion, hoisted the flag of the Rising Sun and sailed out to sea, leaving Fuchida to face the Emperor's questions as to the attack on Pearl Harbor.

Sergeant Jacob DeShazer, stationed on KP duty at the US Air Force base in Oregon, idly listened as hip-swinging jazz tunes and snatches of news about the War in Europe filled the kitchen while he peeled potatoes. Suddenly, he stiffened. Japanese planes had attacked the American Pacific Fleet at Pearl Harbor.

His light eyes blazing and his mouth compressed into a thin line, he listened, stunned, as the casualty list mounted. Eight battleships and ten vessels out of 92 ships had been crippled or sunk; 170 planes went up in flames and roiling black smoke; and 3,700 U.S. officers, soldiers, and military personal had died in the three-hour attack. DeShazer threw a potato against the wall, shouting: "The enemy are going to have to pay for this!" Rage swelled in his chest, making it hard to breathe. He wanted to personally kill as many Japanese as possible. Then came the Bataan Death March—where 10,000 American troops captured by Japanese troops at Corregidor died of starvation and physical abuse—this was the limit. Men, women, and children—nothing was sacred to him anymore since the Japanese atrocities.

In the days and weeks that followed, all he could think of, all he could talk about was a "payback." Reassigned to an air base in South Carolina, he and fellow members of the 17th Bomb Group, volunteered for active duty with a newly-formed unit called "Doolittle's Raiders." Commanded by Lieutenant Colonel Jimmy Doolittle, the Raiders practiced carrier-deck takeoffs, low-level night flying, bombing at low altitude, and over water navigation. At the close of these extensive flying exercises, sixteen crews, including Jacob DeShazer, boarded the carrier *Hornet* for Japan. No one knew exactly the nature of their mission when Colonel Doolittle gathered the crew together in the empty mess hall. The plan, as he put it simply, was "to bomb Japan."

Launched off the deck of naval carriers, 13 bombers would drop their four bombs apiece on Tokyo. The rest of them would hit Nagoya, Osaka, and Kobe. Because of Japanese security measures, no bomber had ever gotten within 500 miles of Tokyo. Since their orders required them to ditch their planes in small fields in China after using up all their fuel for the flight over Japan, the carrier-launched bombers would not be able to return to their carrier once they landed. It was a one-way trip.

Doolittle's famous raid began on April 18, 1942. Japanese intelligence was unable to locate them by radar until two days before they hit. While the American bomber formation headed westward, the Japanese were confident that Tokyo was safe. The Japanese people basked in the golden spring sunshine and the scent of cherry blossoms. No one worried.

B25 lifts off from USS Hornet on Doolittle Raid

Meanwhile, aboard the planes en route to Tokyo, crewmen chalked up slogans like "You'll get a BANG out of this!" Others tied imperial Japanese medals to the bombs ready to blast off. The fun ended when Doolittle announced that Task Force 16 had arrived a day ahead of schedule. They were going in. Doolittle was prepared to take the ultimate risk, but he didn't want to end up a prisoner: "I'm going to bail my crew out and then dive it, full throttle into any target I can find where the crash will do the most good. I'm forty-six years old and have lived a full life."

Detecting two enemy ships by radar while still 700 miles from their goal, the men spent anxious minutes until the "All Clear" signal sounded. The sky was grey with clouds. At dawn, Doolittle climbed aboard the bomber, roaring the engines until they threatened to catch fire. Jacob DeShazer was the bombardier of B-25#16, the plane lovingly called the "Bat." Commanded by Lieutenant William G. Farrow, it was the last of the sixteen B-25s to launch from the *USS Hornet*. At first, it seemed as if they would never get off the ground. Those still out on deck watched tensely, knowing that if Doolittle couldn't make it, even with the help of a stiff wind, they wouldn't make it either. DeShazer's plane struggled to get off the deck, skimmed the water, and then angled up towards the sky, following the bomber formation.

It was 7:20 a.m., just twenty-nine minutes short of the time that Mitsuo Fuchida bombed Pearl Harbor. They approached the green coast of Japan. As they flew inland, they scanned the ground close to see the flash of officers' swords at military bases and people scuttling about like ants. The Japanese Prime Minister, troubled by vague rumors of an enemy force on the island, decided to visit the Mito Aviation School by plane anyway. Just as they taxied onto the runway, a "weird-looking," two-engine craft came into sight. It zoomed past them without firing a shot. As it winged out of sight, the Prime Minister's secretary realized that there had been something strange about the face looking out the pilot's window. It was American.

At 12:30 p.m., Doolittle's Raiders were directly over their target. The Japanese below, out all day for an air-raid drill, thought that this was a sequel to the drilling festivities. Black-haired schoolchildren, mistaking the circular red, white, and blue markings for the spot of the Japanese Rising Sun, waved back cheerfully. No one fired at them. Then the bombs came, falling on the streets in explosions of fire, dust, and brick-work. Circling the Emperor's palace and the hospital grounds, the Raiders dove aside and roared off.

Fuel gauges began to run dangerously low. Straining to reach the Asian mainland, Jacob DeShazer and his B-25 flew straight into the black heart of a storm. They floated in darkness, unable to see either the horizon or the ground below. The rushing 125-mile tail-wind buoyed up the plane, extending the gas' lifetime for a few hours. At midnight, as fuel ran out and a thick fog closed in, preventing any hope of landing, Doolittle's Raiders began to bail out. Parachutes opened with a snap. Deep in the Chinese interior, DeShazer's plane kept going longer than anyone else's. As it faltered, a broad yellow band slipped into sight in the swirling dusk. It was a bend of the Yangtze River—held by the Japanese. Fastening his parachute straps, DeShazer jumped into darkness. The pilot died when he reached the ground. But DeShazer floated for miles in his parachute and crashed.

Doolittle Raiders in China after crash-landing

The force of the impact stunned him. He lay in a tangle of parachute ropes and silk, too numb to feel the sharp twinge of his fractured ribs. When he opened his eyes, he didn't know where he was. Glancing around him in the darkness, he saw it was a Japanese graveyard. Warm April rain poured down, soaking his uniform. Slashing the parachute into bits, he held a piece of silk over his head to keep the rain off. Then he began to walk.

There was nothing here but muddy rice fields. Slipping in troughs of water, catching at crumbly stalks of rice that came away under his grasp, he stumbled and fell. As he opened his eyes, he knew he had to get back to his crew. Staggering blindly along the mud-covered road, he walked straight into a Japanese patrol. The next thing he knew, guards crammed him into a tiny cell surrounded by wooden bars, along with other hapless members of Doolittle's mission. He hadn't eaten all day. Blindfolded and stripped of personal items, he was forced to use a wooden box as a latrine.

The Japanese interrogated him for hours, taunting him with stories about how the Japanese had bombed and taken possession of American territory. They laughed in his face. But he refused to talk. Within the next few hours, he was blindfolded, handcuffed, and deprived of blankets. Cameramen took snapshots as the guards herded them like animals into trucks.

Arriving in Shanghai, blindfolded, handcuffed, and under death sentence, the captives shambled towards the notorious "Bridge House." After sixty days of punishment and deprivation, the men could hardly move. Their shoulder blades and ribs stuck out painfully. Crammed into a 12- by 15-foot cell with fifteen Chinese prisoners, each man received a small cup of boiled rice for breakfast, four ounces of bread for lunch and four ounces for dinner. The guards gave the Americans only two quarts of water per day. Bedbugs, rats, and lice swarmed them in the roasting heat. An additional torture the guards invented was to force them to sit up straight all day. If they even leaned back on their elbows, the guards hit them sharply with bamboo sticks.

One day during this punishment, one of the officers passed out. Some of the men had dysentery, forcing their comrades to carry them to the bathroom every fifteen minutes. When three of the eight Doolittle men had already succumbed to the firing squad, news came that the Emperor had pardoned the rest of the Raiders who bombed Tokyo—including DeShazer.

Back in his cell, DeShazer's body filled with strange joy. He had fully expected death. Instead, he was alive. Even if the war went on for years, he might yet survive. But winter came upon them. The prison was cold as ice, without heat. Some of the enlisted men managed to stay well in spite of it.

Kept on a starvation diet and subjected to brutal treatment, one of the officers, kind and good-humored Lieutenant Robert Meder, became very ill. Soon he was too weak to sit up. Jacob DeShazer could not forget the dying officer's calm face. "He seemed to understand the Bible well. He told me that Jesus Christ is the Lord and coming King; that Jesus is God's Son and that God expects the nations and people to recognize Jesus as Lord and Savior. He said that the war would last until Jesus Christ caused it to stop."

Crouching beside him as he grew weaker, Jacob DeShazer could not understand what he meant. Looking up at DeShazer, Lieutenant Meder pressed his hand against his chest. His heart hurt, he muttered. Then on December 1, 1943, after almost 20 months of captivity, the man Jacob had learned so much from died of starvation. DeShazer knew nothing until heard the sound of hammering next morning. Crawling to look out into the prison yard, he saw the Japanese guards knocking together a coffin. On December 2, Jacob went alone to see Lieutenant Meder's body. He lay in a handmade box with a wreath of flowers, his hands clasping a Bible.

When someone reported the officer's death to the authorities, policy towards the prisoners began to change. The Japanese captain of the prison, knowing Lieutenant Meder had starved to death, asked the prisoners if they wanted anything. Jacob DeShazer surprised himself by asking for a Bible. Finally, in May 1944, he received one. He could only have it, the guard insisted, for three weeks.

As he flipped through its leaves, DeShazer thought of gentle Lieutenant Meder. Meder never hated anyone, even when he lay dying. How was that possible? He knew something of this mysterious Christian love. Across Europe, Africa, and Asia, men killed each other. Civilians died. Americans hated Japanese and Japanese hated Americans. DeShazer's hands trembled with eagerness to find the answer. Chapter after chapter, the words gripped his heart, swallowed him. He read about man's fall from grace and how a Redeemer came to save mankind and restore him to fellowship with God.

By June 8, 1944, he had plunged into the depths of 1 John, and read: "If we confess our sins, He is faithful and just to forgive us our sins and cleanse us from all unrighteousness." Something woke in Jacob DeShazer. Light flooded his soul. Reading the passages about the crucifixion, he saw how Christ suffered. He, too, was beaten, mocked, and tortured, yet he prayed, "Father, forgive them." Bowing his head, Jacob asked God to forgive his enemies as well. He asked for grace to love the men who had killed Lieutenant Meder and locked him in solitary confinement for thirty-four months. Standing at the bars of his cell as water blew in from a tropical rainstorm, Jacob received the rain as his baptism into the faith.

A year passed. Still starved and treated harshly, DeShazer found himself changing despite the fact that his circumstances remained the same. He learned a few words of Japanese. He spoke gently to his guards whenever possible. Soon the men started to treat him with the same kindness. Another hot summer passed into bitter cold autumn. Snow covered the ground, increasing the frailty of the men who had undergone these conditions for almost 40 months.

Suddenly, Spring 1945 blossomed, and American paratroopers dropped from the sky into the Peiping prison compound. Grey and haggard, the men staggered out of prison into blinding sunlight. The war was over—just as Lieutenant Meder had said it would be. As soon as Jacob's plane landed in Washington, D.C., he telephoned his parents on the farm in Oregon. For almost three years, they had no idea if he was alive or dead, only that he was a prisoner. With a cropped prison

DeShazer (left) being released from Peiping prison compound, 1945

haircut, sunken cheeks, and too-bright eyes, he was a walking ghost of the young man who left them to fly the Doolittle Raid in 1942. Now he told his mother, who had prayed daily for his salvation, he wanted to go back as a missionary to Japan.

In 1945, the United States government awarded DeShazer both the Distinguished Flying Cross and the Purple Heart for his participation in the Doolittle Raid. Three years later, with his wife Florence and a degree from the Christian Seattle Pacific College, Jacob DeShazer set foot on the land he had once come to destroy.

On the Yokohama docks, reporters clamored for interviews. How could a man tortured by the Japanese possibly love his captors? Over the next few months, DeShazer spoke in over 200 different places. People wrote to him, thanking him for sharing the gospel. They cried as he spoke of his months as a POW (prisoner of war), unable to comprehend the love God had given him in spite of his circumstances. One girl, whose boyfriend had died in DeShazer's raid on Nagoya, learned he had come to town and determined to kill him. She slipped into the service where DeShazer was speaking, waiting for her opportunity. But forgiveness pervaded DeShazer's messages. The forgiveness of God to man and the forgiveness of men to each other. As she listened, the spirit of God overpowered her, and she broke down and gave her life to Christ.

At a service held in the a theatre in Osaka, Japan, where bombs had fallen in 1942, two of DeShazer's former prison guards pushed forward and asked to receive Christ. Over the next few years, Jacob DeShazer had an opportunity to share the gospel with the Emperor's brother, Prince Takamatsu, and thank the Japanese Emperor for sparing his life. With tears in his eyes, he even led Captain Kato, the man who gave him his first Bible in Nanking Prison, to the Lord.

Then in 1950, the incredible happened. The worlds of Jacob DeShazer and Commander Mitsuo Fuchida collided. Following the attack on Pearl Harbor, Fuchida's life was spared in miraculous ways. The day before the bomb fell on Hiroshima, Fuchida received an unexpected long-distance call from Navy Headquarters, demanding his return to Tokyo. Twenty-four hours later, an atom bomb obliterated Hiroshima.

When the war ended, it took with it Fuchida's entire military career. Discouraged, he went back to his home village near bombed-out Osaka to take up rice farming. As the years passed, he grew older and sadder. Then the war trials came. Summoned to testify before General Douglas MacArthur in Tokyo, he found that no one accused him of war crimes. But the trials investigating Japanese atrocities against POWs reminded him of his lost life, Japan's disgrace in international eyes, and his current reduced status. One day, as the former officer slowly got off the train in Shibuya Station, he saw an American standing on the corner, passing out free literature. As the captain passed by, Jacob DeShazer handed him a pamphlet titled *I Was a Prisoner of Japan*. Great.

Another American who capitalized on the war trials. Just what he needed when he was harassed with inquiries dealing with these very issues. With nothing else to do, he politely took a leaflet and stuffed it in his pocket. Maybe he'd read it later. At home, he took it out and glanced through it. In it, he read an amazing story, the kind of story he hadn't even dreamed about. The story spoke of forgiveness, peace, and love. Fuchida's heart yearned to taste that kind of love. As a child, he had honored his parents according to tradition. In the imperial service of Japan, he did his duty unflinchingly. But no one had ever spoken of love like this.

Commander Mitsuo Fuchida

He looked the tract over carefully. So, the American had found this love and peace in the Bible. As a devout Shintoist and military man, Fuchida had never read the Bible. He went out and bought one. Alone, he devoured the Scriptures for weeks as DeShazer had done years before. The man who had bombed Pearl Harbor without flinching now found himself gripped unspeakably by the story of the Crucifixion. At that moment, he seemed to see Jesus for the first time. He saw not only his crimes against humanity, but his sins against God.

"I was impressed that I was certainly one of those for whom Jesus had prayed. The many men I had killed had been slaughtered in the name of patriotism, for I did not understand the love which Christ wishes to implant within every heart."

On April 12, 1950, Commander Fuchida gave his life over to Christ. His old comrades could not believe their eyes. Again and again, they tried to dissuade him from this "crazy idea," his new-found faith. They mocked him, called him a puppet trying to impress the Americans. Newspaper headlines screamed: "Pearl Harbor Hero Converts to Christianity!" But Fuchida did not care. He had found something worth more than medals and heroism.

Shortly afterwards, Captain Fuchida met Jacob DeShazer. The boy determined to "make the enemy pay" now embraced the lead pilot who dropped bombs on Pearl Harbor. Together, the American POW and the Japanese captain, stiff from war wounds, toured

Mitsuo Fuchida and Jacob DeShazer preached the gospel together throughout Japan after World War II.

the country preaching the gospel. Following World War II, Emperor Hirohito announced to the world that he was not God, for the first time in a thousand years of Japanese history. This admission helped open the way for the gospel to spread in the country of Japan. For Jacob DeShazer and Captain Fuchida, they had come home on angel's wings from the winds of war.

Jacob DeShazer showed forgiveness to his enemies. By returning to the place of his imprisonment with a new heart, he was able to show the love of Christ to people he once hated.

Note: As an elderly man, Jake DeShazer developed Altzheimer's disease. As his memory began to fail him, he remembered preaching to the lost in Japan, but forgot he was ever tortured by them.

Questions

1. What was Jake DeShazer's attitude to the Japanese on hearing of the bombing of Pearl Harbor?
2. Why was Jake DeShazer so eager to enter the service?
3. What part did Jake play in the bombing of Japan?
4. Describe DeShazer's treatment by the Japanese after his capture.
5. How long was DeShazer held and mistreated by the Japanese?
6. Tell how another prisoner's reliance on Jesus Christ impacted Jake's life.
7. Explain how Jake came to give his life to Christ.
8. How did his conversion affect the way he lived while in prison?
9. What did Jake do when released from prison?
10. What evidence in Jake DeShazer's life indicates that he internalized the true meaning of forgiveness?

11. How was God specifically able to use Jake's testimony of forgiveness in the lives of others? Tell of others who received Christ's forgiveness as a result.
12. How do you see the hand of God in the events that occurred concerning Mitsuo Fuchida?
13. Think of anyone in your life that you have struggled to forgive. Remember, God is still working and wants to bring about miraculous situations in your life as well. List anyone you have trouble forgiving. Ask God for the grace you need to experience true forgiveness toward others in your life, and ask God to use you for His greater purposes as He used Jake DeShazer in this amazing story of forgiveness.

Patience

DEFINITION

Waiting for God's timing
by trusting Him

MEMORY VERSE

Wherefore seeing we also are compassed
about with so great a cloud of witnesses,
let us lay aside every weight,
and the sin which doth so easily beset us,
and let us run with patience
the race that is set before us.

Hebrews 12:1

The Bridge on the River Kwai

Colonel Philip Toosey

World War II, Thailand, Malay Jungle

June 1942

Warm tropical rain beat down on their heads as they trudged helplessly through the heavy silence of the Malay jungle. Birds beat overhead and rain poured ceaselessly from the thick, shiny green leaves. Soaked to the skin, they clutched their faded khaki uniforms around them like tattered shreds of dignity. Dirty fingers scooped up bits of rice and stuffed them into mouths, washed down with a gulp of onion water "hogwash" called stew.

Colonel Philip Toosey

"You are going to a health resort," the Japanese said with smiling faces.

They packed up their piano and gramophone records. The Japanese would supply them with gramophones at the resort. Piling their belongings from the Changi prison camp into metal army trucks, the weak, sick, and starving British prisoners set out joyfully on foot.

At the station, short Japanese soldiers in light-colored fatigues began pushing them into line, shouting: "All men marchee, marchee!"

"What?" Somebody asked in dismay. "We're coming for a holiday."

And then the Japanese laughter began, like birds cackling in the jungle.

The defense of Singapore had failed when General Arthur Percival surrendered—the worst defeat in British military history. Thirty-eight-year-old Colonel Philip Toosey, his long face grim, refused evacuation to India. An officer since 1925, he chose to share the fate of his men. Now, on the border between Thailand and Burma, they arrived at the Tha Maa Kham POW (prisoner of war) camp at Tamarkan. Sergeant Risaburo Saito, an army officer in the Imperial Japanese Army, met them in the muddy compound. Looking at the 2,000 British prisoners with something like pity, Colonel Toosey listened as the commandant informed the captured soldiers that they would construct a bridge over the Khwae Mae Khlong (Kwai Yai). The bridge, a feat of Japanese engineering, would create a railway line from Bangkok to Rangoon. Soon Japanese troop trains would pant and whistle across the jungle river into Burma to support the Japanese army.

Toosey, listening carefully, learned that officers would be forced to labor beside their men. According to the rules of the Geneva Convention, the enemy could not use captured officers for manual labor—only supervising duties. The Japanese knew why as well as he. Forcing officers to work would break the authority structure that placed officers in charge of their soldiers. Used as slave labor, officers lost their dignity and their power to give orders. Without authority, an army ceased to exist. Both officers and men would be reduced to the position of slaves.

Work began as the captured men headed into the miserable Thailand winter. Cold rain slid down their backs as they slaved away without shirts. The senior Allied officer on the site, Colonel Toosey walked back and forth, supervising the labor. Patience—patience was the key. If he could keep the men working just enough to allay Japanese suspicion, keep as many men alive as possible, and still sabotage the bridge, then he would have succeeded in thwarting the enemy's plans. A refusal to work amounted to instant execution. But he could do something to delay the bridge and still spare his men. He glanced at the bridge sharply as the Japanese engineers hovered nearby. The men worked with painful slowness. They mixed the concrete sloppily and badly. He studied the steel and concrete monster arching over the slate-grey water beneath the Three Pagodas Pass. The wooden spans supported the huge structure. Suddenly, he had an idea. He gathered his officers together in a little knot and spoke quietly so that the guards would not hear.

Soon the men began overturning and digging under the wet felled trees lying on the hillsides beside the river. Fat white termites grew like mold in the humid air of the jungle. Set free in the cracks and crevices of the bridge, they began gnawing away at the wooden timbers.

In the mud below, a total of 200,000 Asian workers and 68,000 British, Australian, Dutch, and American prisoners worked from the Siam and Burma sides towards the center. Lifting timbers that often broke away and crashed into the water, killing workers, stirring concrete, slapping swarms of mosquitoes, and battling jungle fever, the men worked on. Winter passed and the muggy Thailand summer began as the work edged towards completion in spite of continued British sabotage. By October 1943, 96,000 people had died, over 18,000 of them Allied troops. They called it the Death Railway.

Colonel Toosey also worked patiently in the camp. He strode through the compound, ensuring that discipline prevailed. He battled lice, dysentery, diphtheria, and cholera in his fight to maintain some standards of cleanliness and personal hygiene. Rain gushed down the hillsides and ran continually through the huts in the lower part of camp where the men lay on hard bamboo cots. He made certain that the officers ate meals with their men, establishing deep ties of friendship, unity, and loyalty. The men became as one, a team knit together for survival. Unlike other prison camps, where the officers remained helpless in their efforts to protect their men, Toosey tried to ensure that his men suffered as little as possible. He complained whenever his men were physically mistreated. Each time, the commandant had him repeatedly and brutally beaten. As a skillful negotiator, he also gained favors and better treatment for the POWs.

Willing to suffer for his men, the Colonel organized at least one escape at the risk of his own life. He scraped together a month's rations for two officers. Then he managed to hide the fact of their escape for forty-eight hours—enough time for the men to make their way into the jungle and outdistance the first search parties. When the guards discovered their escape, the Colonel suffered harsh punishment at the hands of the enraged Japanese. Meanwhile, Toosey secretly contacted Boonpong Sirivejjabhandu, a Thai merchant who risked his life to supply the starving prisoners at the southern end of the railway. With his help, Toosey smuggled in quantities of food and medicine from the outside. Mixing medicine, organizing a food supply, and ensuring that work crawled on the bridge, the Colonel instilled hope in his men that they could wait and survive until rescued by Allied forces.

Finally, in October 1943, the Kwai Bridge was completed. Sometime before, the British authorities had determined that such a project would take the royal engineers five years to finish. Now, a gang of soldiers under their patient and courageous officer had built 415 kilometers of bridge and railway from scratch in just 16 months. Both the wooden bridge and the steel bridge stood for two years until blown up during a seventh Allied air raid.

Following the bridge's completion, most of the

The River Kwai bridge as seen from the tourist plaza in Kanchanburi, Thailand

able men moved upriver to new camps. Colonel Toosey stayed behind to create a hospital for the sick at Tamarkan. The Japanese, admiring his area as the best-run prisoner-of-war camp on the Siam-Burma railway, allowed him a high level of freedom. During the last months, they shuttled him around to different camps. He and several other officers were held hostage at Nakhon Nayok when Japan surrendered in August 1945. His weight had dropped shockingly from 157 pounds. He now weighed 105. Despite his weakened condition, he insisted on traveling 300 miles into the jungle to supervise the release of his men. During the post-war trials, Colonel Toosey met Sergeant Saito again. The colonel saved Saito's life when he defended the sympathetic guard against accusations as a war criminal. Through his contact with the British colonel, Saito later became a Christian, stating: "He showed me what a human being should be and he changed the philosophy of my life."

Colonel Philip Toosey demonstrated patience by waiting and working through his present circumstances to save the lives of his men until the situation turned for the better.

For whatsoever things were written aforetime were written for our learning, that we through patience and comfort of the scriptures might have hope.

—Romans 15:4

Questions

1. What had the British been trying to defend?
2. Where were the prisoners being taken? Why was their colonel still with them?
3. What project were the prisoners given?
4. What rule of the Geneva Convention were the Japanese breaking? Why?
5. What was Colonel Toosey's plan to slow down work on the bridge?
6. What hardships did Toosey's men endure?
7. How did Colonel Toosey demonstrate patience?
8. How was Toosey able to help alleviate the suffering of his men?
9. How did he risk his life for his men?
10. What did Colonel Toosey and his men accomplish in 16 months?
11. Why did the Japanese respect Col. Toosey?
12. What did he insist on when he heard his men were being released?
13. Tell of how Sgt. Saito came to be converted.
14. What are some ways you could demonstrate patience in your home? church? neighborhood?
15. Think of a Bible character who demonstrated great patience.

Resourcefulness

DEFINITION

Using creativity to utilize things which others might discard

MEMORY VERSE

And whatsoever ye do, do it heartily,
as to the Lord, and not unto men;
knowing that of the Lord
ye shall receive the reward of the
inheritance:
for ye serve the Lord Christ.

Colossians 3:23-24

Over Enemy Lines

Lieutenant William Overstreet

World War II, France

May 1944

One minute William Overstreet was looking at the altimeter. It flickered at 25,000 feet. The next, an explosion burst near his plane and ripped into his oxygen line, cutting off the flow of air. Far below, Nazi anti-aircraft guns, concealed in the mist and hedgerows, thundered. The heightened compression in the cockpit squeezed the air from his lungs. Suddenly he was swimming in velvet blackness, without sight or sound. Then the P-51C pilot opened his eyes. The brown-and-white Mustang fighter was in a death-spin toward the ground. Clouds whirled and streamed past his window. With a cold emptiness in his ears, he knew that the engine was dead. He glanced at the fuel gauge, which was set to the main tank. It was empty.

P-51C pilot William Overstreet

He didn't know how it happened, but suddenly he came out of the spin. His hands located the switch to the auxiliary fuel tank. Straight ahead, a line of trees rushed up at him from the ground, but then the engine sputtered and roared to life. He side-slipped past the trees, coming down crabwise towards the earth before zooming up again. He glanced at his watch. The past 90 minutes were a blank in his mind. He had flown while unconscious for an hour and a half.

Gaining altitude again, he scanned the green spring fields checkering the French countryside. He had dropped out of flight formation, leaving his squadron commander frantically trying to reach him over the radio. He was alone and lost over German territory. Then his brain kicked in. Simply reversing the direction they had taken towards the mission, he cruised along until he sighted the outline of the French coast. From there, he was home free. He dove off towards Leiston, England, landing at the Fourth Air Base. His gas gauge read almost empty.

Later, flight surgeons at the hospital estimated that he had dropped from 25,000 feet during that lost ninety minutes. If he had remained at the same altitude, he would have died without air in the rarified atmosphere. It had been a close call, but it would not be Bill Overstreet's last.

During flight training at Hamilton Field while assigned to 357th Fighter Group, the twenty-one-year-old Overstreet from Clifton Forge, Virginia, bailed out of a plane in full death spiral just seconds before it crashed in a mass of wreckage.

Later in the war, Overstreet was on a mission escorting bombers to Southern France. Peering through his goggles, Bill spotted the ammunition train looming up at him along the track. Flames and smoke mushroomed into the sky. Shards of metal tore into the plane, shredding its underbelly. He popped open the door, tugged his cord and sailed

The "Berlin Express"

towards the ground where two Nazis were waiting for him. Interrogated by the Gestapo, he found that they knew everything about him. They even knew about his past girlfriends, some before he even joined the military.

"What did my parents have for breakfast?" he demanded.

The Gestapo agent didn't flinch. "I'll tell you tomorrow," he said.

German officers tumbled Overstreet into the backseat of an ammo vehicle. He had to get out of here. If he didn't, enemy soldiers would take him to one of those prison camps for American soldiers and pen him behind rolls of razor wire. One Nazi climbed into the truck and took the wheel. They were a little way into the countryside by now. Just then Bill spotted a pipe wrench lying under the driver's seat. Stooping, he picked it up and tapped the German on the head. Bill pushed the Nazi out of the truck, spun the wheel, and sped off in the opposite direction. He drove until he ran out of gas. On foot now, he located French Resistance partisans who helped him get back to England.

On D–Day, June 6, 1944, Lieutenant Overstreet took off on a mission at 2 a.m. On the ground, the weather was foggy and overcast. After climbing for 20,000 feet, he rolled out on top of a crest of clouds. Moonlight flooded the sky as the planes broke out of the overcast, jutting up at odd angles from climbing so far on their instruments. Teaming up in flights (group of four planes), the pilots winged over to France, covering the beach area so that the massive troop invasion on the ground could land as planned. On the day of the Normandy invasion, Bill and his comrades flew eight missions. On June 10th, he skimmed low to the ground, strafing trains, trucks, and German armored vehicles. Once they had eliminated the enemy ground forces, they were able to claim trains, boxcars, railroad shacks, trucks, lorries, and barges.

Two months later, Bill's group was flying a shuttle mission, a group of U.S. military aircraft missions from one country's base, and then would land

The "Berlin Express" chasing a German fighter beneath the Eiffel Tower

at bases in other allied countries, including Russia. Their task: to escort B-17s from the 8th Air Force's 3rd Bomb Division. It was seven and a half hours across the ravaged steppes of Poland to the ancient city of Cracow. After being engaged in several dog-fights and shooting down two Nazi fighters, the pilots finally bumped gently onto an airfield in Piryatin. While the Russians refueled their fighters, the boys went shopping. Bill became excited when he saw a popular beverage for sale, scarce in war-torn Europe. As soon as he got back to his plane, he dumped all his .50 caliber ammunition and filled the now empty bays with the beverages he'd purchased. Since the next goal was Foggia, Italy, where American troops had fought among the villages and mountains, Bill felt confident that the pilots wouldn't see any Luftwaffe there. Everything went smoothly at first. Then over Romania, the fighter group ran into a pack of German Messerschmitt Bf 109s. But when the Germans saw the Americans, they turned tail and sped for home. Bill was close on the tail of an escaping German plane. Suddenly the German pilot jumped out in a parachute. His plane was not on fire. It had not even been hit. Bill didn't know what had scared the man.

Later, at their debriefing, one of the officers asked: "Who was the closest one to him?"

Everyone grinned. It was Bill, only he didn't have a single bullet on him—his ammo bays were filled with liquid.

On another occasion in Spring 1944, Lieutenant Overstreet pursued a German Messerschmitt through Paris in his fighter, the "Berlin Express." The Nazi, hoping to eliminate the tough captain on his tail, flew straight for the center of the city, where heavy German anti-aircraft artillery aimed their sights at the sky. Several hit the German's engine and enemy flak thudded around Bill. In a last-ditch effort, the German pilot dove beneath the massive, fretwork legs of the Eiffel Tower.

Unhesitatingly, Bill swooped beneath the arch of the Eiffel Tower, flying dangerously close to the ground. He came out of the dive, pounding the German fighter with rounds of ammunition repeatedly. The plane crashed in a blossom of flames. Bill ducked over the Seine River, flying low and on full throttle to avoid heavy flak from the German guns. He followed the course of the river out of Paris.

Asked later what the scenery was like around the Eiffel Tower, Bill replied: "I'm not sure, I was a little busy."

Understatement and modesty would be a lasting characteristic of Bill Overstreet's remarkable career. He demonstrated resourcefulness by making use of the opportunities available to him under stressful situations.

I had followed this 109 from the bombers when most of the German fighters left. We had a running dogfight and I got some hits about 1500 feet. He [German pilot] then led me over Paris where many guns were aimed at me. As soon as he was disabled, I ducked down just over the river (smaller target for the Germans). Followed the river until I was away from Paris.

—William Overstreet

Questions

1. What was Bill Overstreet's assignment in World War II?
2. Tell of his first close call in this story.
3. How did Bill get captured by the Germans?
4. How did he escape?
5. Tell the incredible story of his flying under the Eiffel Tower and shooting down a German Messerschmidt. How did he get away?
6. Tell how Lieutenant Overstreet demonstrated resourcefulness (making use of opportunities others might miss while in stressful situations) in each of these encounters.
7. We often get in a rut of doing things the same way all the time. Resourcefulness is doing things creatively in order to accomplish the task at hand or using things others might discard. How can you train yourself to practice resourcefulness?

Dependability

DEFINITION

Honoring your word and responsibilities even if it means unexpected sacrifice

MEMORY VERSE

He sweareth to his own hurt,
and changeth not... .
Psalm 15:4b

Angels on Omaha Beach

Cecil Breeden

Normandy, France
D-Day, June 1944

Clouds covered the summer sky. The bullets sounded like angry hornets zooming past his head. Zip-zip-zip. In the middle of the heavily-defended German "Green Dog Sector" on Omaha Beach, Cecil Breeden, an Iowa medic, stooped over eighteen-year-old Harold Baumgarten. One of the Company A "Bedford Boys," he lay bleeding heavily on a stretcher on the beach. Shrapnel had slashed his clothes and skin. Moments before, as he lay on the stretcher waiting for evacuation, a German sniper sent another bullet into his body. Soldiers from the 116th Regiment, 29th Division of the

Virginia National Guards Regiment swarmed over the beachhead after the landing ramps went down at the start of the attack. Most of the "Bedford Boys" were mowed down like wheat before the onslaught of German artillery and the carefully-sighted sniper fire. It took four wounds before Baumgarten fell.

As the boy opened his eyes, he could see Breeden's face hovering close above him. The medic did not flinch as German machine-gun fire thudded around him. Instead, he gently treated Baumgarten's wounds before moving off towards the next soldier groaning on the beach. Those watching never forgot the sight. Moving like an angel through a storm of shrapnel and bullets, Breeden passed untouched from man to man, giving help and comfort where he could.

Staring through the cloudy haze on Omaha Beach, Baumgarten knew that God had spared him for some great purpose. If he lived to get off this beach, he would dedicate his life to helping those who needed him as a doctor.

Many of the other "Bedford Boys" were not so fortunate. After a year and a half in England, most of the men would get back into action that summer. Others, with wives and children at home, admitted that they would rather stay in England than assault a beach.

Joining up during the wave of patriotic fervor that broke out in the wake of Pearl Harbor, the "Bedford Boys" vowed, like their fathers in World War I, "to whup 'em good and still be home for Christmas." During the bitter winter of 1942–43, the men trained and struggled to prove themselves, while officers and non-commissioned drill sergeants kept weeding out those who could not make it. Camping out in the driving rain on the Yorkshire fells (mountains), some of the boys found that their Captain Taylor Feller's tough exterior hid a great homesickness. Far from home, many for the first time, the "Bedford Boys" were glad to go with men that they knew. At the same time, they faced criticism from Army regulars who believed that National Guardsmen could only play at soldiers. D-Day would prove them wrong.

As June opened, it brought the birth of Operation Overlord, better known as D-Day, closer. The operation's planners believed that heavy bombing would simply take out the German pillboxes. Craters blown in the sand by the bombing would provide instant foxholes for the soldiers landing on the beach. Then demolition teams would move in to wipe out German officer Erwin Rommel's hidden mines and defenses. Battleships offshore would annihilate anything left. Finally, the first wave of Landing Craft Air tanks, equipped with floating apparatuses, would grind up onto the beach and give them covering fire as the infantry charged in the first assault.

Captain Fellers, listening to the plans and role of the Virginia National Guard in them, began to doubt the success of the operation. They would need a miracle even if everything did go according to plan. Finally, at a military meeting, he could stand it no longer. Despite his rank as a captain, he spoke up.

No one answered.

As Fellers and Lieutenant Ray Nance walked out of the meeting, the captain said quietly, "We'll all be killed, Ray."

Already, Army high command had begun referring to the 116th infantry and Company A as the "suicide wave" that would hit the French beach with the code name of Omaha. Despite his doubts, he remained committed to the operation. Then, just before D-Day, Captain Fellers went into the hospital with a severe sinus infection. Worried, his men crowded on deck, wondering what would happen now. But Fellers met them there.

"I've trained you and I've come to die with you if that's what it takes," he said.

Immediately, the men straightened. "It lifted our spirits to have our leader back," Roy Stevens, one of the Bedford Boys, said.

Their commander stood on the deck as the 29th Division boarded for takeoff. "Are you ready, men?" he asked.

One of them managed to say brightly: "Yes, sir, we're sure ready."

It was dark at 6:30 a.m. when they hit the water, slogging through it with sixty-pound packs weighing on their backs and digging into their shoulders.

Unknown to them, the pilots above them could see nothing due to the blurred cloud-cover. Afraid of hitting their own troops, the planes flew too far inland, dropping the bombs on a few French farms but killing no Germans. Meanwhile, the tanks, equipped with flotation devices, got bogged down in the rear. Some of their own carriers sank, drowning the men on board. The men's hearts sank as they looked out to sea. Now, their only help lay in the battleship *Texas*, as it began shooting rockets towards the beach. Most splashed harmlessly in the water. When the "Bedford Boys" came up onto Omaha Beach, they came alone. There were no foxholes and no covering fire.

Medic treating wounded soldier

Men fell as soon as they hit the beach. Twin brothers, Roy and Ray Stevens, with dreams of owning a farm, stepped off onto Omaha Beach together on that June day. Only one came back. Disaster threatened all of them. Lieutenant Nance, slewing up on the beach in his Landing Craft Air tank, found that the ramp would not go down. Spattered by enemy fire and knowing that the Germans would shoot at the first head that popped up, Nance kept yelling: "GET IT DOWN!"

But the ramp was stuck. Bodies littered the beach. Men stumbling past recognized the prone figure of one of the Hoback brothers. Others saw Earl Parker fall, the man who said he would die gladly if he could only see his little girl, Danny, once more. They never found most of the bodies. Lieutenant Nance, frantically trying to lower his tank ramp, felt it thump to the ground. He lurched up and onto the beach. When he looked behind him, he could not see anyone. Most of his men had gone down within moments of landing. The officer felt sick as he stared down at the carnage. He knew these men. He had trained them personally, watched them grow from raw country boys into top-notch fighters. He felt that he should have somehow protected them. "I felt responsible for them, every last one. They were the finest soldiers I ever saw."

Crawling out of his tank, Nance headed toward a nearby cliff, the only cover visible in the rain of fire. Suddenly, a machine-gun bullet ripped into his heel. As his blood seeped away, the lieutenant stared up at the sky that had just broken into the dawn. It "had a rosy appearance," he said. "A warm feeling came over me and I knew I was going to live."

As he lay near the cliff on Omaha Beach, Nance looked up to see a spotlessly uniformed Navy Corpsman leaning over him. With tender hands, the man dressed the officer's wound. Then he stuck a shot of morphine into his arm.

"This is worse than Selerno," he commiserated. "Good luck to you." Then he disappeared.

Later, when Nance related his experience, everyone told him that he must have had a hallucination. No one could have come off a landing tank under gunfire looking spick-and-span. But Nance showed them his carefully bandaged foot to prove it. If an angel dressed like a Navy Corpsman came to him that day on Omaha Beach, he would always be grateful.

Meanwhile, medic Cecil Breeden moved around the beach on his own errand of mercy, patching up torn bodies without a thought to the ferocious enemy fire. He came through the war and entered Germany without a scratch. He would never receive a decoration for his heroism.

Later that afternoon, a sergeant picked up a weakened Lieutenant Nance and carried him over to an aid station. Lying on the ground, Nance threw out his hand and nearly put it on something that looked like a pie plate.

The sergeant bellowed: "Don't touch it!"

The officer jerked his hand back. He had nearly slammed it down on a German mine. For most of the Bedford Boys, the "Longest Day" was over.

Thousands of miles away, in Bedford, Virginia, families crouched by their radios, listening for news of their boys. None of them knew whether the boys had gone out on D-Day or not. Captain Taylor Fellers, who told his men that he would go out to die with them, died four days later on June 10, 1944.

In total, nineteen Bedford Boys died at D-Day on June 6, 1944. Three more would fall later. Only ten percent of Company A survived the brutal landing without being killed or wounded. A "veil of tears" hung over the quiet little town as wives and mothers mourned the men who had fallen on Omaha Beach. Bedford, Virginia had suffered the heaviest casualties of any community in the United States during World War II.

Cecil Breeden and the other Bedford Boys had shown dependability by doing their duty even if it meant unexpected sacrifice to themselves.

Questions

1. What was Cecil Breeden's job?
2. Who were the Bedford Boys?
3. What was the Bedford Boys' mission?
4. Who was their Captain? Tell what happened to him just prior to D-Day and the choice he made that inspired the confidence of his troops.
5. What types of disaster met the Bedford Boys as they struggled to get to the beach?
6. Tell about how Lieutenant Nance felt observing what was happening to his men.
7. Tell of Nance's injury and how the medic was like an angel of mercy to him.
8. How many of the Bedford Boys survived D-Day?
9. Tell how Cecil Breeden was an incredible example of dependability during this conflict.

Love

DEFINITION

Giving unselfishly in all situations

MEMORY VERSE

My little children,,
let us not love in word,
neither in tongue;
but in deed and in truth.
1 John 3:18

The Flying Panther

Captain Eddie Simpson

World War II, Sens, France

August 1944

The sky was clear. Not a single German Luftwaffe plane zoomed into sight on his tail or beyond the horizon. Twenty-one-year-old Captain K. Eddie Simpson smiled, his clean-shaven face calm, as he shot over the railway target in his P-51 Mustang. A painted black panther, its mouth opened in a snarl and its Pegasus wings spread, soared on the side of the bomber. Just minutes before, the ground crew, consisting of Sergeant Schuenemann, Corporal Petree, and Sergeant Classens, tightly hung a row of bombs under the wings to be dropped like lead balloons onto tracks looking like a child's train set far below.

Eddie Simpson and his crew

The captain had a way of inspiring men to follow him. Other squadron members of the 357th Fighter Group jumped at the chance to fly with him. His friend, Bill Overstreet, noted how Eddie Simpson brimmed over with pleasant good-humor whether at the station in Leiston, England, or in the air flying missions over France.

Simpson, in the lead as one of the 363rd Squadron leaders, slowly swung his craft to the left in an echelon turn as the last bomb fell. Suddenly, something slammed into the "Flying Panther" from behind. First Lieutenant Donald Ferron had fatally misjudged the speed of Simpson's maneuver. The nose of his bomber plowed through the P51's metal skin as fuel burst into flames. As the two planes spiraled towards the ground, locked in a blazing death-embrace, Eddie Simpson bailed out. Farron's plane exploded instantly.

Alone in the clouds, Simpson gripped the straps of his parachute as he drifted towards the earth. Nazi-occupied territory lay just below him. Once he landed, he would have to move fast and silently to avoid capture and death. He dropped and rolled to the ground in a mass of parachute silk. Quickly gathering up the telltale evidence of a landing that would set the enemy on his trail, he started out on foot. He had not gone far when two French Maquis freedom fighters (who opposed the Nazis) slipped out of the woods near Orleans, south of the Loir River. They stared at his uniform. English?

Captain Eddie Simpson

It was the first time that they had met anyone who spoke English except for a few rare British agents. Organized in the attics and cellars of Paris by Jean Moulin (here a man identified only by a closely-wrapped scarf concealing his scarred throat), the French Resistance spread into the countryside. Stealing supplies from Nazi-controlled rail-yards, bombing tracks, killing battalion guards, and running coded messages, the Resistance carried on a desperate underground warfare while the Allies strafed the landscape from above. Led by Colonel Marc O'Neill in southeastern France, the *Maquisards* fought against both the Germans and the pro-Nazi French Vichy government.

Now, Simpson followed the two men into the green depths of the forest. At last, they plunged through the last undergrowth and came in sight of the hidden camp. The band of 300 people staged secret operations against the Germans from their base

Maquis resistance fighters

there. Even their name meant "thicket" or "bush." The Maquis told the captain that he should stay with them rather than try to break through to the Allied lines in the west. Reports had come in that American troops had reached the outskirts of Orleans. In two or three days, they might penetrate far enough into enemy territory for Simpson to link up with them. Eddie agreed to stay.

Days passed in the green-lit forest. The heavy boom of American guns came from the west. The Maquis lived on fruit and berries plucked from bushes, but they feared to hunt for game lest the Germans hear the echo of a gunshot. They also depended heavily on airdrops of weapons and explosives by the British Special Operations Expedition in France (SOE). Every day, the fighters slipped out of camp to engage in lightning attacks on German troops in the area in an effort to keep them from organizing a counter-attack on the advancing Americans.

Eddie Simpson had stayed in camp when the

freedom fighters straggled in at dawn on August 14th. Silently, they laid out the nine bodies of members who had died in a firefight. Eddie took part as the Maquis dug graves deep in the woods near camp to bury their comrades. Just as they knocked in the wooden crosses, a small German patrol broke into the camp on motorcycles. The Maquis leaped for their guns. Under the hail of fire, the Germans swung around and rode off. But it was too late. Their position had been located. Racing back to camp, the Resistance scrambled to pack what they could carry. Leaving instantly, they planned to head north to Paris. There, they would join up with other Maquis units operating near Allied lines.

A mile deeper in the sheltered forest, the Maquis had hidden several captured German trucks. Eddie Simpson followed at a run as the partisans dashed for the vehicles. Grabbing hold of the sides, Eddie hauled himself into the last truck as the motors throbbed. Weaving along a narrow forest track, the Maquis' convoy swung onto the main road leading towards Orleans. As the trucks bumped onto the highway, a large German column with a mass of trucks and armored cars caught sight of them. The roar of motors and squeal of tires accelerated as the Nazis took off after the freedom fighters. Looking at the dust rising behind them, the Resistance knew that the entire unit would be wiped out if they did not do something immediately. They had to stop the

Nazi convoy.

Realizing this, one of the Frenchmen shouted for the driver of Simpson's truck to slow down. As the truck ground slowly to a halt, five Resistance members and Eddie Simpson jumped out of the back of the truck. Grabbing a couple of weapons, they swung a heavy machine gun toward the advancing Germans. Then they gestured to the driver to leave so he could catch up with the convoy.

Scrambling in the dust as the truck raced away, the six men quickly planted the machine gun in the middle of the Orleans road. They crouched, waiting for the German column to come within firing range. As the Nazi trucks roared towards them, the men opened fire. The first slammed to a halt in a mass of perforated metal. With the destroyed vehicle blocking the narrow road near the little village of Ouzouer-sur-Loir, the other German trucks piled up behind the dead truck. They could not squeeze around it.

Members of the Maquis resistance group

Simpson and the others kept firing. But wave after wave of German troops poured out of the trucks. The road was flat and without cover. Within a few moments, Captain Eddie Simpson and the five Maquis freedom fighters lay dead in the road. The "Flying Panther" had completed his last mission. But the rest of the French Resistance had escaped. No one knows why Eddie Simpson sacrificed his life to help men he barely knew, when he could have simply waited for repatriation by the advancing American army. But he did. Eddie Simpson demonstrated true love by giving unselfishly of himself to the needs of others, sacrificing his own life that others might prevail in the war for freedom.

No matter how long it may take us to overcome this premeditated invasion, the American people in their righteous might will win through to absolute victory. I believe that I interpret the will of the Congress and of the people when I assert that we will not only defend ourselves to the uttermost but will make it very certain that this form of treachery shall never again endanger us. ...

With confidence in our armed forces—with the unbounding determination of our people—we will gain the inevitable triumph—so help us God.

—From President Franklin D. Roosevelt, in the December 8th, 1941 speech he gave to Congress after the Japanese attack on Pearl Harbor.

Questions

1. What personality did Eddie Simpson have?
2. What happened that caused Eddie to have to bail out of his plane?
3. By whom was he rescued?
4. What plan was devised to get Eddie back to the American lines?
5. What were the freedom fighters involved in doing?
6. What did Eddie and several freedom fighters do in order to turn the tide of their desperate plight?
7. How were they successful in their mission?
8. Tell how Eddie Simpson portrayed true love in choosing to sacrifice his life for the greater cause of freedom.

Discernment

DEFINITION

The ability to identify
subtle untruths or motives

MEMORY VERSE

For the word of God is quick,
powerful, and sharper than any two-
edged sword, piercing even to the
dividing asunder of soul and spirit,
and of the joints and
marrow, and is a discerner of
the thoughts and intents of the heart.

Hebrews 4:12

The Sub that Sunk a Train

Commander Eugene Fluckey

World War II, Japanese Coast
June 1945

Patience Bay: June 18, 1945. It was 4 a.m. The submarine *USS Barb* hovered in the dark waters off Karafuto, Japan like a glowing green spaceship. Bending over the table, thirty-two-year-old Commander Eugene Fluckey studied the railway line on the map spread out before him. It was Fluckey's fifth patrol in Asian waters, scoring eight direct hits on six enemy ships. Now the Navy wanted to make it his last. Four patrols was the limit before turning over command to a new captain. But Fluckey wasn't about to give up on his men. He was like a father to them. He asked for one last mission, a "graduation patrol," if his fourth proved a success. Admiral Lockwood had agreed. For almost six weeks the *Barb* cruised the seas, annihilating Japanese coastal defenses and supplies. They called him "Lucky" Fluckey. He had another name, too: "The Galloping Ghost of the China Coast," for his speed and daring vanishing acts. By July 18, Fluckey had worked up his finale. They were going to attack a train.

Commander Eugene Fluckey

If they could blow up the main railway line running inland from the coast, the damage might halt the enemy advance in that region for days or even a week. Smiling, he rubbed tired, creased eyes. In the next compartment he heard excited chatter, the high tenor of young men and the deeper tones of the older men sitting around in their undershirts. The men knew about the upcoming strategy, but only that they planned to destroy the rails.

Straightening up, Fluckey walked through the sub to the control room, something he did several times a day. He liked to talk to the men, to gauge their mood and gain their perspective at the height of a mission. He knew each of the eighty men aboard by name. He asked them about their wives and families, which baseball team they liked best, or where they went to school.

A person had to get used to living in a sub. The cramped space and lack of sunlight created inevitable tension among men new to the business of covert warfare. But these men were seasoned veterans. If a submarine had to dive to avoid *akikazes,* fast, low-lying Japanese minesweepers, the world suddenly became a closed torpedo, floating in lightless subterranean depths. There were nerve-wracking minutes when the *Barb* had to surface during a chase due to shallow water. Unable to dive, the submarine would skim along the surface of the coastline, heading out to sea with Japanese gunboats in full pursuit. If the *Barb* were hit by a Japanese sub, the crew wouldn't stand much of a chance swimming out of the wreckage alive.

But Fluckey wouldn't trade this life for a comfortable desk job behind the lines. Other submarine commanders lost their subs or their lives in the China seas, but Fluckey, with a curious blend of discretion and daring, had kept intact and afloat through five missions. Now as he faced a cluster of officers and men, he dropped the bombshell. Not only were they going to blow up the rails, but they had to time the detonation for the instant that one of the Japanese supply trains passed, without blowing their own shore patrol sky high. The men nodded at each other. This sounded like "Lucky" Fluckey, the tough submarine commander and recent recipient of the Medal of Honor. Fluckey warned them of the risks involved. It was a comparatively easy task to dynamite a railway line and a harder one to hit a train in motion without killing the men sent ashore. But by avoiding reckless actions, they could do it. "We don't have problems," he stated calmly, "only solutions."

1147: "Battle Stations!"

Too late now to discuss ways and means. A Japanese freighter appeared on the horizon, accompanied by a pack of frigate escorts. It drew closer, its steel prow looming up out of the water, big and menacing. On the upper deck, Commander Fluckey peered at it through his binoculars. Little black figures swarmed the ship's bridge.

1200: "Hitting time."

The bowshot technique—setting off a bomb underwater straight into a vessel's bow—was a last-ditch effort. The freighter exploded, the Rising Sun

U.S.S. Barb

flag blowing into the air. By noon, the frigate lay in pieces on the ocean floor. When the Japanese learned of the wreckage by radar, the *Barb* would become a hunted ship. A Soviet ship trailed them for a time before turning aside.

1807: *"Dive! Dive!* Plane closing fast, nine miles."

Enemy planes circled overhead. Cruising slowly beneath the surface, the *Barb* spent an hour unable to come up for air. Fourteen hours had passed since the first decision to blow up the supply train and they still hadn't figured out the logistics.

Bill Hatfield, an electrician from West Virginia, spoke up. "I've one idea."

Fluckey nodded. "Let's have it."

According to Hatfield, they had to bury a 55-pound high-explosive charge under the track to catch both track and train. The bomb was big, over a foot long and wide, so they had to dig a hole and sandwich it between two ties. Then they could bury the batteries wired to it in a nearby hole and activate the charge. Then to complete the circuit, the engineers would hook in a microswitch. Placed on the surface between the next two ties, the switch would do the job.

The Commander listened intently. "Sounds simple enough, but please explain to us simpletons just how do we set off the microswitch?"

"You don't, sir. The train does."

"Okay. How?"

Bill grinned. "The rail sags underneath the weight of the engine. So we mount the switch on two wedges, slip it under the rail, the engine comes along, the rail sags, closing the switch, and she blows!"

Fluckey clapped Hatfield so hard on the back that he staggered. The idea was perfect, discreet, and did not pose such a threat to the lives of his men. But they still had to figure out how much the rail sagged. It depended, Bill said, on the size of the engine. Japanese engines were about one-third the size of American ones, so it would take less impact to explode the charge.

"When I was a kid," Hatfield said excitedly, "we used to crack nuts that way. Oh, I'd say the rail sags enough to crack a good-sized black walnut laid on a hunk of wood."

"How much is that?"

Hatfield pinched together his thumb and forefinger. "About yea big."

Fluckey decided "yea big" was about an inch. It would work.

One of the crewmen appeared. "Captain, we're still submerged and twilight is ending."

Fluckey nodded. "Take her up."

They would use rubber boats. But enemy frigates still hovered near the coast and the *Barb* sensed radar interference from all of them. The Commander stalked back and forth.

"Jim, we can't get ahead of them unless they

leave that coast. Nor can we surface in this bright moonlight without being gunned."

He stared through the night periscope as the frigates sailed out to sea. Then he turned the sub around and headed back for Patience Bay. The train was now top priority. Still, Fluckey worried about the crucial amount of give in the railroad ties. An overestimate could cause the risky operation to fail. As for an underestimate, he did not even consider the possibility. Though his eyes pricked with sleep, Fluckey went to his cabin, hauled out a thick book of engineering, and started scribbling equations. It was a long night. When the lieutenant came to the door of Fluckey's cabin, he found the commander sound asleep, his head resting on his arms. The engines throbbed quietly as the *Barb* drifted through nighttime seas.

2337: "Captain, contact. Showing Soviet lights."

"Keep clear, Bill."

Morning came. As they cut across Patience Bay towards the western shore, Fluckey shut his cabin door and drew the curtains to draw up the list of men for the sabotage party. Lieutenant Bill Walker, the biggest and strongest officer on board, would lead the mission. All types, from electricians, motor machinists, and torpedo-men to the lead cook had a fair chance to serve. Only married men could not go. If the party had to flee and survive under critical conditions, it would be through the mountains of northern Karafuto to the Russian part of Sakhalin Island.

Satisfied, Fluckey left his cabin to tell the men. They watched as he singled out the marine commandos. Detailed to land as a shore patrol, these men would carry out the operation while the *Barb* covered them from a distance. Fluckey refused to unnecessarily risk his men's lives, but he did want to blow up that train. As the names rang out, men stepped out by twos and threes and stood aside. Faces clouded with disappointment as reality sank in: only eight could go ashore. The selected party beamed when informed they were to go.

Quietly, the commander finished: "I'll lead the saboteurs. This isn't a combat situation, yet it's too risky to turn over to someone else. I'm sure I could pull it off."

One of his officers stopped him. "Sir, I swear I'll send a message to ComSubPac if you attempt this. It's not in the best interests of the men."

Reluctantly, Fluckey agreed. "I suppose you're right, but I hate to miss this once-in-a-lifetime opportunity."

For the next few days, the men trained and gathered equipment. Seamen strapped on combat gear and inflated lifejackets. Weapons lay in rows for test runs. They even had a waterproof firing system for wet weather. In his cabin, the Captain double-checked his equations for mistakes. The rail sag was 1/10 inch. Every few hours, he took a quick walk through the boat to check the pulse of the sub.

Everyone was calm, peaceful. Those who didn't get to go gave helpful suggestions. Suddenly, someone mentioned the danger of attack dogs.

Fluckey sent for a Japanese prisoner nicknamed "Kamikaze." Rolling his expressive black eyes, Kamikaze said that Japanese guards patrolled the cliffs, rocks, beaches, and villages. On foot, they passed at a regular interval of two hours, night and day. Sometimes they had two guards, usually one. Carrying pistol and rifle, they always kept a dog close by their side. The patrols' purpose was to keep Soviet spies off the island. The captain told the men to carry a few steaks apiece to throw to the dogs. That was better than trying to fight them.

Fluckey spoke again to the crew. Only one man must approach the rails to make the final live connection. While he stooped to do that, all the others must lie down flat on the ground at least twenty yards away. Keep exposed body parts turned away and eyes closed. He didn't want anyone killed or blinded by the flash if there was a mistake. For four days, they scanned the sky. They needed a moonless night. Or a night with drifting clouds that threatened to cover the moon. As soon as the cloud blotted out the white disk, the commandos could move in. In the meantime, the submarine lay still. The sea must lie perfectly quiet, lulled into a false sense of security, before the attack.

During that time, the engineers built the

microswitch the train would trigger as it passed over. A team went down to the boiler room and cut up steel plates. Heating the sheets to white-hot temperatures, they bent and shaped the metal into picks and shovels. The work done, the men waited anxiously. Only five days of their patrol remained. They had to act now or never.

1837: They dove and observed the island. When they surfaced, it was bright moonlight. Cloudless. They cruised softly around, looking for a lone sampan—a native boat—that they could capture to help the men in landing. On the submarine deck, the commander watched the sky. But days passed, and still their chance did not come.

July 21: Dawn spread over the twin peaks of the green mountains visible further inland. This would be their guide for paddling in. Crewmen brought the *Barb* in to less than 1,000 yards from the beach by radar before the commandos disembarked. Meanwhile, the engineers built a test circuit to iron out any kinks. The men's spines tingled with anticipation.

July 22: Commander Fluckey, standing on lookout in the early twilight, scanned the two green peaks. White cirrus clouds capped the mountains, wreathing their heads in dense white fog. Slowly, a luminous cloud bank drifted across the sky, piling up behind a three-quarters moon. Fluckey turned to the men. Tonight was the night.

The party could return no later than 0230 and twilight commenced at 0245. A sampan, looking like an ancient basket, floated along the beach while the *Barb* hooted at the moon. Softly, the men communicated with each other as they launched the rubber boats. When one group approached the other, it let out a low, clear whistle: "Bob white!"

Fluckey listened to the signal for assembly, the liquid cry of the American whippoorwill.

"Ti-la-ti."

He prayed that the Japanese wouldn't know their bird calls and suspect foul play. The men practiced communication in the final moments. A blast on a whistle meant an emergency dash for the boats. Two lights sprinkling the sky signaled, "We are in trouble."

Fluckey had some final words with Lt. Bill Walker. If the spot isn't good or the odds poor, don't risk it. Bring the men back immediately. Move with discretion. Make sure every man has meat to throw to the dogs. Booby trap the train. Slip in and out again. Do not be detected. He looked into Bill's eyes. Most importantly, bring the men out alive.

Flooded by moonlight, the *Barb's* silhouette looked like a Spanish galleon floating on a golden sea. In the dark of the moon, the Japanese would not see the boats from shore. No one would dream that a submarine could swim so close in such shallow water. The men clambered down, noiselessly inflating the rubber boats. There was a quiet jostling, the tinkle of equipment.

Nighttime raids suited Fluckey best. He loved slipping through the water under cover of darkness. Sleek, torpedo-grey sharks cut through the cove, driving silvery swirls of fish before them. Sharks were the original torpedoes, built for speed and silence, their dorsal fins jutting at a ninety-degree angle. They could lurk underwater, surfacing in a flash to grab a fish or a man's leg. In this nautical underworld, the *Barb* glided through Karafuto Bay like a giant beast of prey.

2230: Radar detected. Small boats came down the coast, zigzagging towards them. They passed safely.

July 23/0000 hours: "Launch the boats." The commandos went in, silently dipping their oars. Fluckey, heart beating, listened for the sound of shouting, shots, the spurt of a flare. Nothing reached his ears. There was only thick darkness. The boats scraped up on the beach. No lights glimmered anywhere. It was a primitive feeling, like the dawn of time. His thoughts went to the men hiding in the bulrushes, to Bill. Bulrushes crackled and snapped at every move. The men of one party, moving forward, ran into each other. Someone reached for a throat, nearly strangling the man before he saw it was a friend. Whispers raw with anger and relief, hissed among the bulrushes. "Why didn't you give the signal?"

"My throat got dry."

They were digging feverishly on the railroad ties when a man came running up to Bill. "Captain, a train is coming up the track!" No!

There was no light except a faint red glimmer from the firebox. White smoke swirled out behind like a magician's cape. No wonder they had not seen the train coming until it was almost on top of them. The Japanese were masters at blacking out trains, concealing every crack of light. The boys must be smack in the middle of digging the battery hole.

Bill sweated copiously. "I hope the holes in the track don't send the train careening off the rails. This could ruin everything."

A glow like a red eyeball went by on the track. As it passed in a rush of hot wind, the men pressed their ears to the rail, listening. No sound. The crew scurried back to work. No sooner had they begun again, the breeze from north to south roaring in their ears, than they heard a train bearing down on them less than eighty yards away.

The men panicked. Bill jumped clear of the tracks and into a briar patch. They lay flat on the ground as the train roared by, the engineer leaning out of the cab and staring at them. But nothing happened. No alarm bells went off. When the second scare had passed, the men raced to finish the holes in twenty minutes. Soft whippoorwill calls floated across the night air. If something happened to a commando, the next man knew how to take over the job.

Crew of the U.S.S. Barb

Now the moment came. Nobody wanted to hide in the bushes. They all wanted to see Bill complete the final step. With seven men breathing down his neck, Bill Hatfield began connecting the live switch. Somebody said, “It won’t work.” Another reached down and patted it till Bill rasped, “Stop it, before you blow us all to kingdom come!”

The switch connected. Leaving the tracks, the commandos headed for the beach through the swaying clumps of bulrushes. The group softly whistled “Bob white” twenty yards away from the boats where the others crouched.

1045: Train coming. The men leaped into the boats and paddled fast. White smoke enveloped the tracks.

1047: Boom! Wham! The charge blew the engine into the air. Boilers exploded, creating flying wreckage, cars cracking and writhing. Orange and blue flames lit the horizon. Silence for several seconds. Then came the snapping and grinding sound of tortured steel. Commander Fluckey, standing on the deck of the submarine, heard it. He swept the area with his binoculars as the *Barb* swung out to sea. They were alone.

The men pulled the rubber boats close for boarding as their fellow crewmen pulled them up. Hatches sprang open. There were shouts, cheers. They had done it. A large Japanese supply train had gone up in smoke.

Safe on board the ship, the men began singing "Down the Valley." And as the submarine purred out towards the open sea, Fluckey could hear them shout again and again: "Hear the *Barb* blow!" It was a night neither he nor the United States Navy would ever forget. In total, Commander "Lucky" Fluckey destroyed more gross tonnage than any other submarine commander in the Pacific theatre. More importantly, the expedition at Karafuto Bay was the only instance that American troops set foot on Japanese soil during World War II.

Eugene Fluckey demonstrated discernment by carefully choosing trustworthy and knowledgeable men to use for the job in order to not endanger their lives and to assure the accomplishment of their mission.

Our debt to the heroic men and valiant women in the service of our country can never be repaid. They have earned our undying gratitude. America will never forget their sacrifices. Because of these sacrifices, the dawn of justice and freedom throughout the world slowly casts its gleam across the horizon.

—President Harry S. Truman, April 16, 1945, following the death of President Franklin D. Roosevelt

Questions

1. What was the purpose of this mission Commander Fluckey was leading?
2. How did he feel about his men? How did he treat them?
3. What idea did Bill Hatfield come up with to accomplish the mission?
4. Why was this mission especially dangerous to his men?
5. What type of weather were they waiting for before attempting the mission?
6. What type of signal did they use to communicate with each other?
7. Was their mission a success?
8. For what was it distinquished?
9. How did Commander Fluckey demonstrate the virtue of discretion?
10. How can you best avoid any actions or words that would give the appearance of evil in your life?

Deference

DEFINITION

To hold others in esteem
and give them first choice

MEMORY VERSE

Let nothing be done through strife
or vainglory; but in lowliness of mind
let each esteem other
better than themselves.
Philippians 2:3

Sun-Swept Afternoon of Horror

Lieutenant Adrian Marks

Workd War II, The Philippine Sea
August 1945

They had ordered him never to land the frail seaplane on the high seas, only on water as calm as glass. But as twenty-eight-year-old Lieutenant Adrian Marks stared down at the tiny figures barely floating on the dazzling hot sea, he could not turn his face away. No boat lay in sight. Looking around at his eight crewmen, he knew that they could all die if he touched down on those choppy waters. But he had to try.

Sailing solo through the Philippine Sea from Guam, where it delivered the first operational atomic bomb to the island of Tinian, the *USS Indianapolis* made its return trip with 1,200 men aboard. At midnight on Sunday, July 29th, a Japanese submarine skipper, Lieutenant Commander Mochitsura Hashimoto, spotted the giant vessel cruising through the sea. Immediately, he sent six torpedoes hurtling through the water. Two crashed into the ship's side. Explosion after explosion rocked the *Indianapolis.* As it pitched over in the darkness, Navy signalmen frantically radioed SOS's. Rolling over on its side, the *Indianapolis* sank in twelve minutes. Over 400 men died instantly. Another 800 leapt into the water as the distress signals blinked through the night.

USS Indianapolis

Due to a Navy oversight, the commanders of the Pacific Fleet did not worry when the *Indianapolis* did not show up at Leyte Gulf in the Philippines three days later. On a hot, glittering sea infested by sharks, the survivors clung to bits of wreckage throughout Monday, Tuesday, and Wednesday. Bruised, dehydrated, and burnt by the sun, the men paddled more slowly as hours stretched into days.

Then on Thursday, August 2nd, at 10 a.m., Lt. Wilbur C. Gwinn, flying a routine flight, looked down and saw them. Of the 800 men who had initially survived the Japanese torpedo attack, only 317 remained alive. Lieutenant Adrian Marks, radioed from the nearby island of Peleliu, arrived first on the scene in his PBY5A Catalina plane, nicknamed "Dumbo." On what he later called "a sun-swept afternoon of horror," he began dropping life-rafts to the men later that day. One shattered as it struck the high, cresting waves.

This was not working.

Then the lieutenant turned to his crew members. Should they disobey their strict orders and make a dangerous and possibly fatal landing on the open sea? One by one, they all agreed to try. The mass rescue began.

Dropping straight from the sky, Marks touched his plane down between crashing, twelve-foot swells. The plane bounced hard, shooting fifteen feet into the air when it hit the water. But the impact only shook and battered the little craft. It did not crack up. As "Dumbo" rode the waves towards the scattered groups of survivors, the officer and his men came to a "heartbreaking decision." They could not save everyone. Squinting at the glassy surface of the sea, the lieutenant decided that the men huddled together

PBY-5-A Catalina

could stay afloat the longest. In waters filled with the darting shadows of sharks, these men could stick together and splash and shout to scare the killers away. Painfully closing his heart, Marks headed towards a single man barely treading water. The crewmen tossed him a life ring at-

Lieutenant Adrian Marks

tached to a rope. Then they circled for another, bouncing on the heavy waves. After a little while, two men lay on each bunk in the seaplane. Others packed two and three deep in every compartment. Finally, when breathing room became cramped, Marks switched off the engines. Then he helped more survivors onto the bouncing wings, lashing the last of them down with strips of parachute silk. He had saved 56 men.

A warm tropical night pressed down on the sea. A high wind whipped up. Behind him in the bunks and compartments, Marks could hear dozens of men moaning in pain. They had run out of their last drop of water hours ago. Suddenly, a light pierced the darkness on the far horizon. The bulkhead of a destroyer, *Cecil J. Doyle,* loomed out of the sea. The first of seven rescue ships sent late to the scene, the *Doyle* spotted the little seaplane, its wings weighed down by drooping men and its engine silent, bobbing helplessly on the waves. Sailors pulled the survivors on board. Then they helped a tired Lieutenant Marks and his crewmen aboard as well. Later that night, the *Doyle* cruised around the Philippine Sea, picking up scattered survivors.

The next morning, Marks watched as the destroyer sank his seaplane, "Dumbo," too badly damaged to ever fly again. Twelve days later, Japan surrendered. World War II had ended. The survivors of the *USS Indianapolis* had weathered the worst maritime disaster in the history of the American navy. Lieutenant Adrian Marks never let himself forget what he had seen on August 2, 1945. Afterward, Admiral Chester Nimitz, the commander of the Pacific Fleet, would pin the air medal on the young officer. Thirty years later, at a reunion of the *Indianapolis* survivors, Adrian Marks looked the men in the eye and said: "I met you on a sparkling, sun-swept afternoon of horror. I have known you through a tropical night of fear. I will never forget you."

Adrian Marks demonstrated deference by setting his own comfort and safety aside to rescue others in need.

I met you on a sparkling, sun-swept afternoon of horror. I have known you through a tropical night of fear. I will never forget you.

—Lieutenant Adrian Marks

Questions

1. What mission had the *USS Indianapolis* just completed?
2. Where was the ship headed when it was attacked?
3. What is the name of the Japanese lieutenant who torpedoed the *Indianapolis?*
4. How long had the survivors been in the water when rescued?
5. How many men survived the ordeal?
6. What were some of the dangers being in the water so long?
7. What brave decision did Marks and his men make that was against orders? How was he later rccognized for his deference?
8. What did Marks and his men do when their plane ran out of room?
9. What ship came to transport the men to safety?

Bravery

DEFINITION

Standing alone for righteousness and yielding my fears to God

MEMORY VERSE

"Have not I commanded thee? Be strong and of a good courage; be not afraid, neither be thou dismayed: for the Lord thy God is with thee whithersoever thou goest."
—Joshua 1:9

From Pastor to Spy

Dietrich Bonhoeffer

Berlin, Germany • World War II
April 1945

World War II was raging. Hitler had crossed a line. Many of his own generals began to view him as a madman who must be stopped. A plot began to form to put an end to his evil atrocities. As a result, Dietrich Bonhoeffer, a devoted pastor, was faced with life-and-death decisions.

During the 1920s, Germany was reeling from the reparations imposed on it by the Treaty of Versailles. These reparations were payments forcing Germany to reimburse the Allies for war damages incurred during World War I. Inflation was out of control, people were saddled with vast economic hardships, and the whole structure of their government was unstable. Citizens desperately sought someone who could offer them some hope. The conditions were ripe for a person with evil intentions, promising false hope, to grab the reins of power. Adolf Hitler, aspiring to dominate the world, was that man.

In 1933, Hitler, with his cleverly concealed motives, was elected chancellor. This was one of the highest government offices in Germany. He was now the Führer or leader of Germany. He gave promises to lead the country out of all its troubles and make it a great nation again.

Days later, Dietrich Bonhoeffer, a 26-year-old pastor deeply committed to the gospel of Jesus Christ, spoke out against potential problems that often arose from such leadership. He warned against idolizing the Führer. He explained that true leadership gets its authority from God, but the Führer answered to no one. He reminded Christians that governments were established by God for law and order.

Bonhoeffer's speech, for some unknown reason, was instantly cut off. The broadcast never finished. The speech, however, was published in the newspaper, and he was invited to deliver it in its entirety at a college. He preached with passion: "The church has only one altar, the altar of the Almighty . . . before which all creatures must kneel. The church has only one pulpit, and from that pulpit, faith in God will be preached, and no other faith than the will of God, however well-intentioned."[1] The freedom to speak so openly would soon be cut off.

Dietrich Bonhoeffer

Dietrich Bonhoeffer was facing a moral dilemma. He felt inaction in the face of evil was wrong. He was a preacher, committed to the gospel of Jesus Christ. He instructed Christians that the Church is the Church only when it is helping others. It should not dominate others but serve. To live for Christ is to live for others. He knew there were many others opposed to the growing deception occurring in the German church. In May 1934, he and other church leaders met in Barmen, Germany. There, they voted to establish the Pastors' Emergency League, which would publicly separate them from the German Christian Church, now run by Hitler. The Pastors' Emergency League was committed to a Church grounded in the teachings of the Bible as opposed to the corrupt theology now propagated by Hitler. Hence, the Confessing Church was born. Its goal was to "confess" the real Jesus in the face of the false German church.

On June 29th, 1934, Hitler, as the chancellor of Germany, unleashed a widespread murder spree called the "Night of the Long Knives." Close to 1,000 people were slaughtered, some even dragged from their beds and forced to face a firing squad. Hitler lied, saying those slaughtered were part of a coup... He explained his actions this way: "In this hour I was responsible for the fate of the German people, and thereby I became the supreme judge of the German people . . . everyone must know for all future time that if he raises a hand to strike the State, then certain death is his lot."[2]

Hitler began to tighten his grip on power through deceit and propaganda. He issued orders to limit citizens' freedoms, including their right to express opposing opinions. Houses were subject to search at any time, and possessions could be confiscated for any reason. Phone calls or letters were no longer private. Political enemies were arrested in the streets, and many were killed, tortured, or imprisoned. Hitler even convinced Parliament to give him the ultimate authority to eliminate its own existence. He proclaimed that the German race was a special race destined by God to overthrow all its enemies. Many desperate German people were taken in by his message.

In 1935, Bonhoeffer decided to establish seminaries to train pastors devoted to the Bible, even though Hitler outlawed them. Bonhoeffer started with 23 students. He found a building in Zingst on the coast of Germany. The school soon outgrew the building and moved to Finkenwalde, now a part of Poland. Many families were sympathetic to his cause, and the community pitched in to help in many ways.

Hitler declared himself the supreme authority of the German church and ordered every pastor to take an oath of allegiance to Hitler personally. He told them he had been appointed by God to be their "Savior", and thus the Reich Church was established.

When the president of Germany died, Hitler combined the office of chancellor with president and proclaimed himself ruler. He had the military take an oath of loyalty and unconditional obedience not to the German nation or constitution, but to himself.

Hitler instituted a policy known as the "Aryan Paragraph," which stated that all government jobs must be held by people of Aryan or European heritage. Any people of Jewish heritage had their jobs immediately terminated. Nazi storm troopers (nickname for German paramilitary) hit the streets to stop German people from shopping at Jewish-owned businesses. Jewish lawyers and doctors were no longer allowed to practice. Dietrich wrote a paper entitled, "The Church and the Jewish Question" to help German Christians clarify how to respond biblically to such treatment of the Jews.

Hitler abolished all political parties other than the Nazi Party. Books written by any author other than German ones were burned. No one could print, publish, or distribute the Bible. No Bibles or crosses were allowed. Crosses were replaced with the swastika, the Nazi symbol. Adolf Hitler was now truly Germany's dictator.

In 1937, more than 800 Confessing Church pastors and leaders were arrested or imprisoned. During the year, Bonhoeffer taught a seminary course at Finkenwalde while finishing up a book on the Sermon on the Mount entitled *Discipleship*. It became one of the most influential books of the 20th century. By the end of the summer, the seminary was forced to close its doors. Bonhoeffer devised a plan to continue training men with the help of pastors belonging to the Confessing Church. Bonhoeffer is famous for having said, "Silence in the face of evil is itself evil. Not to speak is to speak. Not to act is to act."[3] He was burdened for the suffering Jewish population.

About this time, Hitler held a meeting with his generals, laying out his strategies to attack multiple countries in his master plan for world domination. Several generals left the meeting shocked, convinced that Hitler was a madman who must be stopped. This was the turning point for many. They resolved to find a way to assassinate him.

On November 9, 1938, Hitler's full-fledged war on the Jewish people broke out in what became known as the "Night of Broken Glass." He gave orders for the Jewish population to be terrorized. Jewish businesses were burned, synagogues torched, and Jewish people beaten and killed in the streets. Soon, Jews, gypsies (Romani people group), political enemies, and anyone who opposed Hitler were rounded up by special soldiers and transported to concentration camps. The camps had been secretly established to annihilate "undesirables." Men, women, and children were herded into trains and taken there. Most of the camps used gas chambers to kill people. The guards lined people up, telling them they would be taken to "bath houses" to shower. Instead of water, poison gas would spray out of the faucets. At one camp, as many as 2,000 prisoners could be killed per hour. Some people were shot, others hanged, and still others used for gruesome medical experiments. Later, this mass killing became known as The Holocaust. The camps were supposed to be secret, so bodies were disposed of by burning them in huge ovens. Over the course of the war, over six million people were killed in these camps. "In 1933, there were about nine million Jews in Europe. By the time the war ended, two out of every three Jews had been killed. One and a half million of them were children."[4]

Bonhoeffer learned from his brother-in-law, Hans, a member of the German Military Intelligence, that two attempts had been made by high-ranking military officials to assassinate Hitler but had failed. Hans was secretly involved in the conspiracy against Hitler. Hans' boss Admiral Canaris supported what he was doing and asked Hans to record what he called "The Chronicle of Shame." It was used later as evidence of the atrocities being perpetrated upon innocent people. The Nazi's brutal ways were beyond comprehension. Dietrich was appalled by what he heard. How could human beings do such horrible things to other human beings? Canaris suggested a way that Dietrich could help. "He would join the agency as a double agent spying on his home country. To the Nazi government, he would appear to be a loyal agent, working to gain secrets abroad for the Third Reich, in the guise of a normal pastor. In reality, he would be just the opposite, a resistance worker under cover as a Nazi pastor, trying to smuggle information to the Allies about how to defeat Germany and Hitler himself."[5]

This put Bonhoeffer in a sensitive position. He had to use the utmost secrecy, and his fellow pastors in the Confessing Church did not understand what he was doing. His main job was to give support and encouragement to those more directly involved. However, Bonhoeffer came to believe that "doing nothing would be just as evil as helping the Nazis do their terrible deeds."[6]

Dietrich continued his church work and writings. *The Prayerbook of the Bible* was the last book he wrote. It was a courageous criticism of Hitler's effort to abolish anything Jewish. He boldly published a book about the Psalms to encourage Christians. It did not go unnoticed by the Nazis.

On April 5th, 1943, Bonhoeffer was taken to Tegel Military Prison, suspected of taking part in a conspiracy against Hitler, although they had no proof. He would never return home. "Dietrich quickly became quite a curiosity at Tegel Prison. The guards all felt his presence there to be a bit bizarre. He just didn't fit in with the mold of the other prisoners; he was measured and kind. He seemed to be buoyed by a kind of inner strength that the others, even the guards, longed to possess. Dietrich became kind of an unofficial pastor to the entire prison."[7]

He used the time in prison to write hundreds of letters, poems, and theological writings. Finally, in July 1943, he was told the charge against him: evasion of military duty and assisting others to do the same. He began to hope he might be released. But then a letter was uncovered which showed that Bonhoeffer had known about the attempts to kill Hitler. Therefore, he would be held guilty of conspiracy.

He was loaded into a van and transported to Buchwald Concentration Camp. There, he was appalled by the sight of the skeleton-like prisoners. On April 8, Easter Sunday, fellow prisoners asked him to conduct a church service. He chose 1 Peter 1:3 as his text. As he was finishing his short sermon, the door burst open. He was told to come with the guards. One of his fellow prisoners took him by the hand and said perhaps they were just moving him. Dietrich shook his head and, smiling calmly, said, "This is the end. But for me, it is the beginning of life."[8]

He was taken to Flossenburg Concentration Camp, where he was tried for treason. It had been almost exactly two years to the day since he was first incarcerated. The following day, he and five other prisoners were hanged on the gallows and their bodies burned. The camp doctor told of his death: "Through the half-open door in one of the huts I saw Pastor Bonhoeffer kneeling on the floor praying fervently to his God. I was most deeply moved by the way this lovable man prayed, so devout and so certain that God heard his prayer. At the place of execution, he again said a short prayer and then climbed the steps to the gallows, brave and composed. His death ensued after a few seconds. In the almost fifty years that I worked as a doctor, I have hardly ever seen a man die so submissively to the will of God."[9]

His family did not hear about his death until the end of May. Those who loved him remembered words he'd spoken in a letter to Confessing Churches: "Who can comprehend how those whom God takes so early are chosen? Does not the early death of young Christians always appear to us as if God were plundering his own best instruments in a time in which they are needed most? Yet, the Lord makes no mistakes. Might God need our brothers for some hidden purpose on our behalf in the heavenly world? We should put an end to our human thoughts, which always wish to know more than they can, and cling to that which is certain. Whomever God calls home is someone God has loved.[10]

In the words of Bishop Bell, who conducted Bonhoeffer's memorial service, "Wherever he went and wherever he spoke, he was fearless, regardless of himself, and with it all, devoted his heart and soul to his parents, his friends, his country as God willed it to be, to his Church, and to His Master. The blood of the martyrs is the seed of the Church."[11] Bonhoeffer's selfless acts of bravery to stand alone for righteousness in the face of persecution still serve to inspire believers today to fearlessly uphold the truth of God's Word against evil.

Questions

1. What was the cause of instability in Germany after World War I?
2. What did Dietrich Bonhoeffer believe about the responsibility of government?
3. Name multiple instances in which Bonhoeffer demonstrated bravery in the face of evil.
4. How did Bonhoeffer provide leadership for fellow Christians?
5. Why did Bonhoeffer feel it was the right thing to do to oppose Hitler?
6. How did Bonhoeffer put others above his own safety?
7. What did Bonhoeffer believe about keeping silent in the face of evil?
8. How did Bonhoeffer stand out as being different while a prisoner?
9. Is there any area of your life that you need to address with bravery?

Selected Bibliography

Andreyev, Ivan. *Russia's Catacomb Saints: Lives of the New Martyrs*. California: Saint Herman of Alaska Press, 1982.

Bashkiroff, Zenaide. *Nights Are Longest There: A Young Girl's Account of Revolution in Russia*. London: M. Spearman, 1960.

Berkin, Carol. *Revolutionary Mothers: Women in the Struggle for America's Independence*. Vintage Press, 2006.

Bruce, Philip Alexander. *Brave Deeds of Confederate Soldiers*. Harrisonburg: Sprinkle Publications, 2006.

Caldwell, Charles. *Memoirs of the Life and Campaigns of the Honorable Nathaniel Greene, Major General in the Army of the United States and Commander of the Southern Department in the War of the Revolution*. Philadelphia: Robert Desilver, printer, 1819. Reprint. Nabu Press, 2010.

Callo, Joseph. *John Paul Jones: America's First Sea Warrior*. Naval Institute Press, 2006.

Cheripko, Jan. *Caesar Rodney's Ride Eighty Miles for Freedom*. Boyd's Mill Press, 2004. (Grades 3-6).

Davis, Burke. *To Appomattox: Nine April Days, 1865*. N.Y: Rinehart & Company, 1959.

Delaplaine, Edward S. *Francis Scott Key: Life and Times*. Heritage Books, 2011.

Driggs, Laurence La Tourette. *Heroes of Aviation*. Little, Brown and Company, 1918 (Armand Pinsard).

Elliot, Elisabeth. *A Chance to Die: The Life and Legacy of Amy Carmichael*. Revell Press, 2005.

Fluckey, Eugene. *Thunder Below! The USS "Barb" Revolutionizes Submarine Warfare in World War II.* University of Illinois Press, 1997.

"The Flying Panther: Captain Edward J. Simpson." *American Aviation Society*, 2011.

Fougara, Katherine Gibson. *With Custer's Cavalry*. Iyer Press, 2007.

Franklin, Benjamin. *Benjamin Franklin's Autobiography.* W.W. Norton & Company, 1986.

Franks, Norman, and Harry Dempsey. *Nieuport Aces of World War I. Osprey Aircraft of the Aces*, No. 33. Osprey Publishing, 2000 (Armand Pinsard).

Gaustad, Edwin S. *Liberty of Conscience: Roger Williams in America.* Judson Press, 1999.

_______________ *Roger Williams*. New York: Oxford University Press, 2005.

Gilmer, George R. *Sketches of Some of the First Settlers of Upper Georgia, of the Cherokees, and the Author.* New York 1855, 1926, p. 90 (Reprinted in 1965 by Genealogical Publishing Co., Baltimore, and 1989 by Heritage Papers, Danielsville, Georgia).

Goodyear, Robert C. *The Real Pennsylvania Dutch American, "Molly Pitcher": A Documented History.* Author House, 2012 (Suggested reading).

Grack-Koestler, Rachel A. *Molly Pitcher: Heroine of the War for Independence*. Chelsea House Publications, 2005.

Green, Roger. *The Life and Ministry of William Booth: Founder of the Salvation Army*. Abingdon Press, 2006.

Hattersley, Roy. *Blood and Fire: The Story of William and Catherine Booth and the Salvation Army*. New York: Doubleday, 2000.

Hearn, Chester G. *Tracks in the Sea: Matthew Fontaine Maury and the Mapping of the Oceans*. International Marine Press, 2003.

Hembree, Charles R. *From Pearl Harbor to the Pulpit: The Dramatic Story of Captain Fuchida and Jacob DeShazer*. Akron: Ohio, Rex Humbard World Wide Ministry, 1975.

Hocker, Edward W. *The Fighting Parson of the American Revolution: A Biography of General Peter Muhlenberg, Lutheran Clergyman, Military Chieftain and Political Leader*. Philadelphia, PA: Edward W. Hocker, 1936.

Holt, Rackham Vincent. *George Washington Carver: An American Biography*. New York: Doubleday, 1963.

Hull, Michael D. *Peter Francisco: American Revolutionary War Hero. Military History Magazine*, July-August, 2006.

Kackley, Paul. "The Dead Yank Hero of Orleans Forest." *Stars and Stripes*, 25 Nov. 1959.

Kalpaschnikoff, Andrei. *A Prisoner of Trotsky's*. New York: Doubleday Page, 1920.

Kidd, Thomas S. *Patrick Henry: First Among Patriots*. Basic Books, 2011.

Knight, Lucien. *Georgia's Landmarks, Memorials, and Legends*. Penguin Publishing, 2006 (Nancy Morgan Hart).

Lewis, Meriwether. *Original Journals of the Lewis and Clark Expedition, 1804-1806*. New York: Arno Press, 1969.

Littauer, V. S. *Russian Hussar*. London: J. A. Allen, 1965.

Marks, Lara. "Sacagawea as an Evolving Symbol of American Indian Women." Dec. 16, 1998.

Marshall, Charles. *An Aide-de-Camp of Lee*. Kessinger Publishing, 2007.

Muhlenberg, Henry A. *The Life of Major-General Peter Muhlenberg, of the Revolutionary Army*. Philadelphia: Carey and Hart, 1849.

Perry, John. *Sergeant York: His Life, Legend, and Legacy: The Remarkable Untold Story of Sergeant Alvin C. York*. Barnes and Noble Books, 1997.

Phelps, M. William. *Nathan Hale: The Life and Death of America's First Spy*. Thomas Dunne Books, 2008.

Polsky, Michael. *The New Martyrs of Russia*. Montreal: The Saint Job of Pochaev Brotherhood, 2002.

Ramage, James A. *Grey Ghost: The Life of Colonel John Singleton Mosby*. University of Kentucky Press, 2009.

Rappleye, Charles. *Robert Morris: Financier of the American Revolution*. New York: Simon & Schuster, 2010.

Salisbury, Gay and Laney Salisbury. *The Cruelest Miles: The Heroic Story of Dogs and Men in a Race Against an Epidemic*. New York: W. W. Norton & Company, 2005.

San Souci, Robert D. *Kate Shelley: Bound for Legend*. Dial Books for Young Readers, 1995. Scott, Jane. *A Gentleman as Well as a Whig, Caesar Rodney and the American Revolution.* University of Delaware Press, 2000.

Scott, John Thomas. "Nancy Hart: 'Too Good Not to Tell Again.' "*Georgia Women: Their Lives and Times*, vol.1. Chirhart, Ann Short, and Betty Wood, Ed. Athens: University of Georgia Press, 2009.

Silcox-Jarrett, Diane. *Heroines of the American Revolution: America's Founding Mothers.* Scholastic, Inc., 2000 (Lydia Darraugh).

Skeyhill, Tom. *Sergeant York and the Great War*. The Vision Forum, Inc., 1998.

Snow, William P. *Lee and His Generals*. New York: The Fairfax Press, 1982.

Strachey, Lytton. *Queen Victoria: An Eminent Illustrated Biography.* New York: Black Dog & Leventhal Publishers, 1998.

Summers, Julie. *The Colonel of Tamarkan: Philip Toosey and the Bridge on the River Kwai*. London: Simon & Schuster, 2005.

Thomas, Evan. *John Paul Jones: Sailor, Hero, Father of the American Navy.* New York: Simon & Schuster, 2003.

Vaughan, David J. *Give Me Liberty: The Christian Patriotism of Patrick Henry* (Leaders in Action). Cumberland House Publishing, 2002.

Walker, Gary C. *Civil War Tales: Volume II.* A & W Enterprise, 1994.

Washington, Booker T. *Up from Slavery.* New York: Dover Publications, 1995.

Waters-Power, Alma. *Virginia Giant: The Story of Peter Francisco.* New York: E.P. Dutton, 1957.

Wellman, Sam. *George Washington Carver: Inventor and Naturalist.* Barbour Publishing, 1998.

Wetterer, Margaret K. *Kate Shelley and the Midnight Express.* Scholastic, 1990.

Williams, Roger. *A Plea for Religious Liberty* in: *The Bloudy Tenant of Persecution.* Providence, Rhode Island: Narragansett Club, Vol. III, 1867.

Wrangel, Peter N. *Always with Honor.* New York: Robert Speller and Sons, 1957.

Websites

"Bill Overstreet." http://www.cebudanderson.com/billoverstreet.htm

"Bill Overstreet, 363rd FS." http://www.cebudanderson.com/overstreet.Htm

"Bill Overstreet: Barnstormers." http://www.barnstormers.com/eFLYER/2009/061-eFLYER-FA02-Legends-Overstreet.html

Winstead, Jane. "Horatio G. Spafford: The Story Behind the Hymn 'It is Well with My Soul.' " http://voices.yahoo.com/horatio-g-spafford-story-behind-hymn-is-1620793.html?cat=38.

Image Credits

Bravery

Bonhoeffer in his Berling garden in 1939: https://en.wikipedia.org/wiki/Dietrich_Bonhoeffer#/media/File:Bundesarchiv_Bild_146-1987-074-16,_Dietrich_Bonhoeffer.jpg

Deference

Lieutenant Adrian Marks: Public Domain. Clinton County Historical Society, http://srv1.geetel.net/~cchsm/lt__cmdr__adrian_marks.htm

USS Indianapolis: public domain; http://www.secondworld-war.org.uk/indianapolis.html

PBY-5 Catalina: http://www.zenithpresstheblog.com/2010/04/military-snapshots-pby-5-catalinas.html.

Dependability

Medic treating wounded: Public Domain. http://www.usmessageboard.com/education/120085-today-isthe-66th-anniversary-of-d-day-june-6th-1944-a.html

Discernment

Eugene Fluckey: Public Domain. http://www.history.navy.mil/photos/pers-us/uspers-f/e-flucky.htm.

Photo #: NH 103534

USS Barb: http://www.history.navy.mil/photos/sh-usn/usnsh-b/ss220.htm. Photo #: 19-N-83952

USS Barb crew: http://www.history.navy.mil/photos/sh-usn/usnsh-b/ss220.htm. Photo #: NH 103570

Forgiveness

Jacob DeShazer: all photos: Public Domain. http://en.wikipedia.org/wiki/File:DeShazer.jpg official USAF photo. http://www.pellfamily.com/sermons/DeShazer3.jpg

Doolittle Raider taking off from USS Hornet: http://www.history.navy.mil/photos/images/g40000/g41196.jpg

Doolittle POW/Chinese: http://ww2db.com/image.php?image_id=6494 National Archives and Records Administration

Doolittle raiders in China: http://ww2db.com/images/battle_doolittle22.jpg National Archives and Records Administration

POW photo DeShazer: Photo by USAF

Mitsuo Fuchida: Public Domain. http://en.wikipedia.org/wiki/File:MitsuoFuchida.jpg

Fuchida and DeShazer: Public Domain. http://www.gerhardy.id.au/images/fuchida&deshazer.gif

Honor

Gen. Pyotr Wrangel: all images: Fair Use. (Image taken from http://www.trio.ru/antika/belarmy/vrangel.htm (historic photo of a famous individual, reduced in size))

White Army exodus from Crimea: http://zolotoivek.tumblr.com/post/12860602362/russian-exodus-fromcrimea-1920

Love

Capt. Eddie Simpson and his crew: Public Domain. http://www.cebudanderson.com/simpson.htm

French resistance fighter: http://ww2total.com/WW2/Weapons/Infantry/Firearms/British/Sten-Gun/images/French-resistance-fighter-with-Sten-px800.jpg

French resistance marching in mountains: http://festungenthirdreich.devhub.com/blog/587799-partisanwarfare/#comments

Evacuation of Novorossiysk,: Новороссийская эвакуация норм 1.jpg, Wikimedia.

Patience

Col. Philip Toosey: copyright The Toosey family Collection http://en.wikipedia.org/wiki/File:Philip_Toosey_1942.JPG

The River Kwai bridge photo: https://upload.wikimedia.org/wikipedia/commons/2/24/Bridge_on_the_River_Kwai_-_tourist_plaza.jpg

Punctuality

Gunnar Kaasen: Public Domain. http://en.wikipedia.org/wiki/File:Gunnar_Kaasen_with_Balto.jpg

Togo: Public Domain. http://merriemarie.livejournal.com/212859.html

Balto: Public Domain. http://perrofeliz.net/perros/la-carrera-del-suero-a-nome-y-sus-protagonistas/

Resourcefulness

William Overstreet, Berlin Express: Public Domain. http://www.cebudanderson.com/overstreet.htm

Berlin Express/Eiffel Tower: http://www.davidmaloney.com/ebuilder/mar10/overstreet.htm

Lieutenant William Overstreet Jr., 363rd Fighter Squadron 357th Fighter Group

Endnotes

1. Eric Metaxas, *Bonhoeffer: Pastor, Martyr, Prophet, Spy* (Nashville, TN: Thomas Nelson Publishers, 2015) 57.
2. Ibid. 89.
3. Ibid. 118.
4. Ibid. 202.
5. John Hendrix, *A Faithful Spy* (New York: Abrams Fanfare, 2018) 102.
6. Metaxas, *Bonhoeffer: Pastor, Martyr, Prophet, Spy* 143.
7. Hendrix, *A Faithful Spy* 132.
8. Dayspring MacLeod, *Dietrich Bonhoeffer—A Spoke in the Wheel* (Scotland, UK: Christian Focus Publications, 1973) 151.
9. Metaxas, *Bonhoeffer: Pastor, Martyr, Prophet, Spy* 212.
10. Janet and Geoff Benge, *Dietrich Bonhoeffer: In the Midst of Wickedness* (Seattle, Washington: YWAM Publishing, 2012) 205.
11. Metaxas, *Bonhoeffer: Pastor, Martyr, Prophet, Spy* 218.

About the Authors

Marilyn Boyer is the mother of fourteen children, all home schooled from kindergarten through high school. Her passion to train up her children in the character of Christ led her to create Character Concepts Curriculum, a character curriculum for kids of all ages to equip parents in raising children of integrity!

Her many character resources, as well as books on homeschooling and Christian parenting, are available online.

About the Authors

Grace Tumas Ehrman holds a degree in history from Liberty University. Her paper, "Warlords and Samurais: Japanese Interventionists in Siberia During the Russian Civil War, 1918-1922," won an award at the 2013 Phi Alpha Theta History Conference. She specializes in American and Russian history.

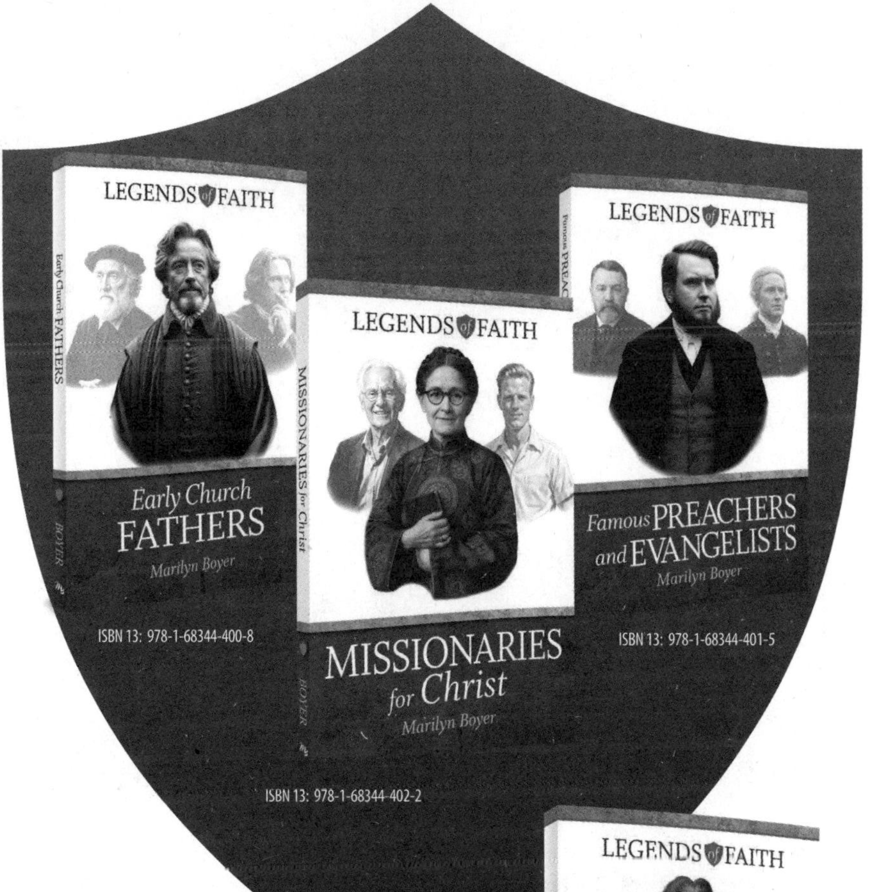

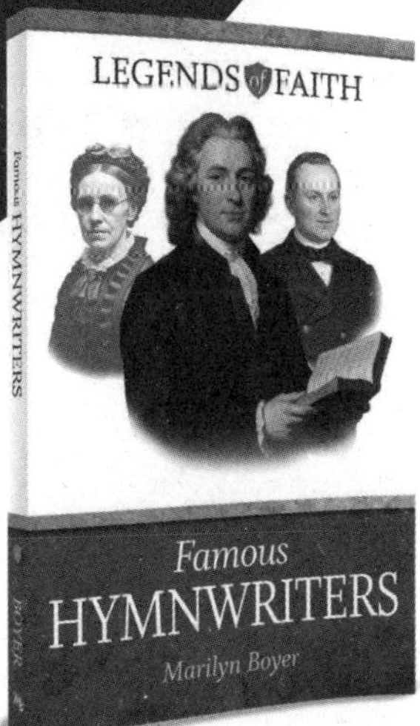

What a Character!
READERS FOR KIDS
Notable Lives from History
Inspire Students with Biographies of Notable Lives from HISTORY.